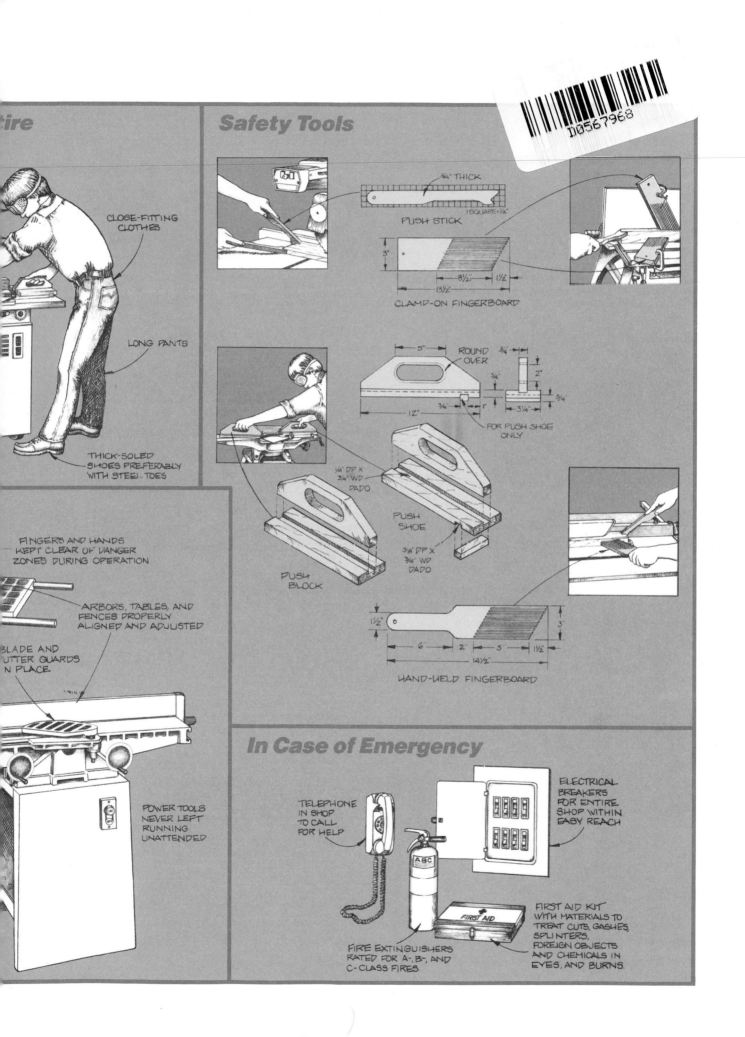

...ire

Safety Tools

CLOSE-FITTING CLOTHES

LONG PANTS

THICK-SOLED SHOES PREFERABLY WITH STEEL-TOES

FINGERS AND HANDS KEPT CLEAR OF DANGER ZONES DURING OPERATION

ARBORS, TABLES, AND FENCES PROPERLY ALIGNED AND ADJUSTED

BLADE AND ...UTTER GUARDS ...N PLACE

POWER TOOLS NEVER LEFT RUNNING UNATTENDED

3/4" THICK

PUSH STICK

1 SQUARE = 1/2"

3"

8 1/2"   1 1/2"

13 1/2"

CLAMP-ON FINGERBOARD

5"   ROUND OVER   3/4"

3/4"   2"

12"   3/4"   1"   3 1/4"   3/4"

FOR PUSH SHOE ONLY

1/4" DP X 3/4" WD DADO

PUSH SHOE

3/8" DP X 3/4" WD DADO

PUSH BLOCK

1 1/2"   3"

6"   2"   5"   1 1/2"

14 1/2"

HAND-HELD FINGERBOARD

In Case of Emergency

TELEPHONE IN SHOP TO CALL FOR HELP

ELECTRICAL BREAKERS FOR ENTIRE SHOP WITHIN EASY REACH

ABC

FIRST AID

FIRE EXTINGUISHERS RATED FOR A-, B-, AND C- CLASS FIRES

FIRST AID KIT WITH MATERIALS TO TREAT CUTS, GASHES, SPLINTERS, FOREIGN OBJECTS AND CHEMICALS IN EYES, AND BURNS.

·BUILD·IT·BETTER·YOURSELF·
WOODWORKING PROJECTS

Closets, Chests, and Boxes

Collected and Written
by Nick Engler

Rodale Press
Emmaus, Pennsylvania

Copyright © 1991 by Rodale Press, Inc.

All rights reserved. No part of this publication may be reproduced or transmitted in any form or by any means, electronic or mechanical, including photocopy, recording, or any other information storage and retrieval system, without the written permission of the publisher.

Printed in the United States of America on acid-free ∞, recycled paper

If you have any questions or comments concerning this book, please write:
Rodale Press
Book Reader Service
33 East Minor Street
Emmaus, PA 18098

Series Editor: Jeff Day
Managing Editor/Author: Nick Engler
Editor: Roger Yepsen
Copy Editor: Barbara Webb
Graphic Designer: Linda Watts
Graphic Artists: Mary Jane Favorite
                 Chris Walendzak
Photography: Karen Callahan
Cover Photography: Mitch Mandel
Cover Photograph Stylist: Janet C. Vera
Proofreader: Hue Park
Typesetting by Computer Typography, Huber Heights, Ohio
Interior Illustrations by Mary Jane Favorite and O'Neil & Associates,
  Dayton, Ohio
Endpaper Illustrations by Mary Jane Favorite
Produced by Bookworks, Inc., West Milton, Ohio

Library of Congress Cataloging-in-Publication Data

Engler, Nick.
    Closets, chests, and boxes / collected and written by
Nick Engler.
        p.   cm.—(Build-it-better-yourself woodworking
        projects)
    ISBN 0–87857–947–8 hardcover
    1. Cabinet-work.   2. Storage in the home.   I. Title.
    II. Series: Engler, Nick.   Build-it-better-yourself woodworking
projects.
TT197.E52 1991
684.1′6—dc20   91–8423
                                                         CIP

8 10 9 7   hardcover

Contents

A Place for Everything

*T*hink of this the next time you retrieve something from a closet or a drawer: What stands between us and chaos, between civilization and anarchy, is a concept so brilliant that it deserves to be included with fire and the wheel as one of mankind's most important achievements. Yet it's often overlooked because of its simplicity — the humble *box*.

Long before mankind needed a place to sit, eat, or sleep, it needed a place to keep its stuff. We put off the invention of the chair, table, and bed to devise small storage containers from woven grasses, bark, or hollow limbs. In these we kept the first primitive trappings of civilization — a few stone tools, dried meats and fruits, an extra pair of deerskin mittens.

By 2700 B.C., the Egyptians and Mesopotamians had accumulated more stuff than anyone else, and were making wooden boxes with metal hinges to keep it in. Concurrently they created the first woodworking joints. At first they sewed the boards together with leather thongs, much the same way their ancestors had woven pieces of bark together. Over several hundred years of box-building, they developed much of the sophisticated joinery we still use today. Boxes became more varied, more elaborate — and more numerous.

They also became bigger. Around 500 B.C. ancient Greece had collected more stuff than either Egypt or Mesopotamia, and so became the beacon of Western civilization. The *kiste* (from which we get the word *chest*) was the principal piece of furniture in most Grecian households. This was a large box with a fitted lid, used principally for storage. On occasion, it probably did double duty as a table, bench, or bed, particularly in humbler households. Some Greek chests were works of art, fitted with elaborately worked metal hardware, painted or inlaid panels, and carved legs and moldings.

The chest remained the most important piece of household furniture for almost two thousand years. Peasants hollowed out logs and fitted them with lids to make crude storage chests. Nobles and knights nailed together riven planks to make six-board chests, bound them with iron straps, and painted them with Latin mottos and coats-of-arms. Immigrants traveling to the New World generally took just one piece of furniture with them — a chest.

But even as Europe began to colonize America, many folks had outgrown their chests. The Renaissance brought improved methods of work and production, and this generated more stuff — so much stuff, in fact, that people were no longer content just to store it. They needed to *organize* it as well. Joiners, as woodworkers were then called, began to build chests with *drawing boxes* (drawers) and *cupboards* with shelves. The upper class began to build homes with small rooms called *wardrobes,* forerunners of the modern walk-in closet.

During the next few centuries, the Industrial Revolution precipitated an avalanche of material goods. Elaborating on the ancient chest, woodworkers created chests of drawers, china cabinets, linen presses, pie safes, bookcases, and armoires, and many other storage devices. By the turn of the twentieth century, folks were erecting homes with *permanent* storage areas, adaptations of the old wardrobe — closets, pantries, kitchen cabinets, and a variety of built-in cupboards.

That avalanche continues today, with no sign of abating. And woodworkers continue to rise to the challenge, devising new and different closets, chests, and boxes to keep our stuff from overwhelming us.

Shaker Knife Box

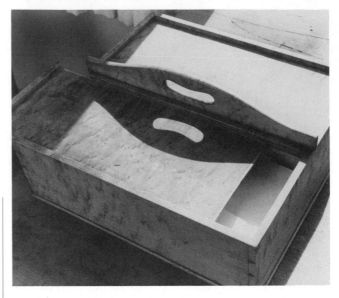

Early American settlers often stored eating utensils, sewing notions, hand tools, and similar items in small boxes they could easily carry from place to place. This portable knife box is one example. It was made in the early nineteenth century by the members of the Union Village Shaker community near Lebanon, Ohio, and has been used constantly for almost two hundred years to store and transport small items. Currently, it serves to organize in-going and out-going mail.

Traditionally, knife boxes from this era had sliding lids. This particular box has *two* such lids — and two separate compartments. The divider between the compartments also serves as a carrying handle.

The parts of the box are joined with decorative mitered dovetails. The top pins and tails are mitered, while the rest are ordinary through dovetails. When viewed from above, the miters form a frame for the lids.

Materials List

FINISHED DIMENSIONS

PARTS

A.	Sides (2)	$5/16''$ x $3^3/4''$ x $11^1/4''$
B.	Back	$5/16''$ x $3^3/4''$ x $10^1/2''$
C.	Front	$5/16''$ x $3^1/8''$ x $10^1/2''$
D.	Bottom	$1/4''$ x $10^3/4''$ x $11^1/2''$
E.	Divider	$5/16''$ x $5^1/2''$ x $11^1/4''$
F.	Lids (2)	$1/4''$ x $4^{13}/16''$ x $10^{15}/16''$
G.	Guides (2)	$5/16''$ x $5/8''$ x $11^1/2''$
H.	Pulls (2)	$5/16''$ x $5/8''$ x $5^3/32''$

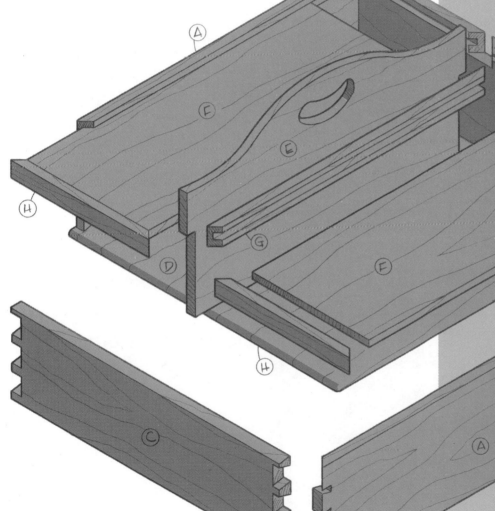

EXPLODED VIEW

HARDWARE

$7/8''$ Wire brads (24–30)

1

Select the stock and cut the parts to size. To make this project, you need about 2 board feet of 4/4 (four-quarters) stock. Because the parts of the box are thin, they should be made from a hard, stable wood, such as maple or cherry. The Shakers often made small pieces from *figured* hardwoods. The original antique knife box is made from maple.

Resaw the stock in half, then plane the pieces to $5/16''$ thick. Cut the sides, back, front, dividers, guides, and pulls to size. Miter the ends of the guides and pulls. Glue the stock edge to edge to make the wide board needed for the bottom. Let the glue dry for at least 24 hours, then plane the bottom and the remaining $5/16''$- thick stock to $1/4''$. Cut the bottom and lids to size.

2

Join the front, back, and sides with dovetails. As mentioned earlier, the back and sides of the box are joined with *mitered* dovetails. The top pins and tails are wider than usual, and the top $5/8''$ of these are mitered for decoration, as shown in the *Back-to-Side Joinery Detail*. The lower tails and pins form ordinary through dovetails. The front and sides are joined in the same manner, but the mitered tails of the front are missing. The front is cut so the top edge sits $5/8''$ *lower* than the top edges of the sides, as shown in the *Front-to-Side Joinery Detail*.

Make both the mitered dovetails and the through dovetails at the same time. Carefully mark the tails (both mitered and regular) on the sides, as shown in the *Dovetail Layout*. First cut the mitered tails in the back top corners of the sides, sawing the miter and then the shoulder of each piece. (See Figures 1 and 2.) Cut

the mitered surfaces in the front top corners of the sides in the same manner. Then make the ordinary tails. Cut the sides of each tail, and remove the waste with a chisel. (See Figures 3, 4, and 5.) Use the tails to mark the pins, then repeat the procedure. Cut the mitered pins, saw the sides of the regular pins, and remove the waste with a chisel. (See Figures 6, 7, and 8.) Fit the joints together.

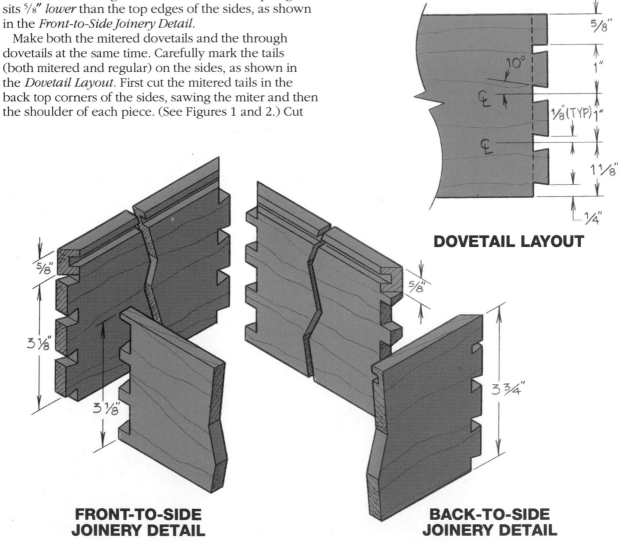

DOVETAIL LAYOUT

FRONT-TO-SIDE JOINERY DETAIL

BACK-TO-SIDE JOINERY DETAIL

1/When making a mitered dovetail joint, make the mitered tails first. Using a dovetail saw, cut each miter down to the shoulder.

2/Still using the saw, cut the shoulder.

3/Next, cut the sides of the ordinary tails down to the baselines. **Note:** Cut on the **waste** sides of the lines.

4/Remove the waste between the tails with a chisel. Use the chisel alternately as a cutting tool and a wedge. First, cut down about $1/16$" along the baseline.

5/Then place the point of the chisel on the end grain of the waste, about $1/16$" from the top surface. Lightly tap the chisel with a mallet until a small amount of waste splits off. Repeat until you have removed all the waste from between all the tails.

6/Use the completed tails to mark the pins on the front and back.

7/Repeat the same procedure. Cut the mitered pin, then saw the sides of the ordinary pins. Once again, cut on the **waste** sides of the lines. Remove the waste between the pins with a chisel.

8/Slide the pins and tails together. Because you cut on the waste sides of the layout lines, the fit should be tight. If it's too tight, shave a small amount of stock from the pins with a chisel until the parts slide together smoothly. The mitered faces should butt together with no gaps.

3

Cut the shape of the divider. Enlarge the pattern in the *Divider Layout,* then lay out the shape of the divider on the stock. Cut the outside shape with a band saw or scroll saw. To make the cutout for the handle, drill two ½″-diameter holes through the waste, about 2″ apart. Remove the stock between the holes with a scroll saw or saber saw. Sand the sawed surfaces.

4

Cut the grooves in the sides, back, guides, and pulls. The lids slide in and out of ¼″-wide, ³/₁₆″-deep grooves in the sides, guides, and back. In addition, the pulls are grooved to fit over the front ends of the lids. Cut these grooves with a table-mounted router or dado cutter.

TRY THIS! The lids should fit snugly in all the grooves — even those that you want them to slide into. Later, you'll scrape or sand the lids so they fit a little looser.

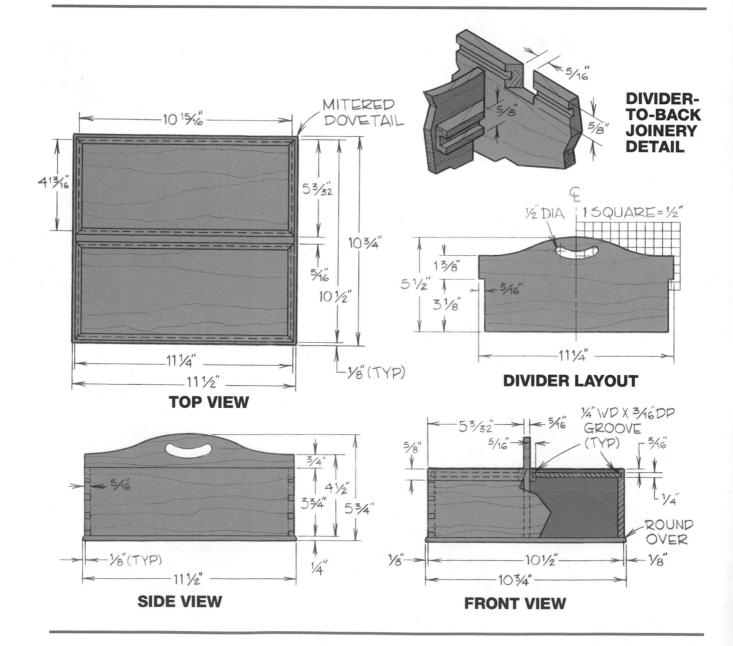

DIVIDER-TO-BACK JOINERY DETAIL

TOP VIEW

DIVIDER LAYOUT

SIDE VIEW

FRONT VIEW

5

Miter the ends of the guides. The back is notched for the divider, and the sides of the notch are mitered to fit the guides, as shown in the *Divider-to-Back Joinery Detail.* Lay out the notch, then cut the mitered sides with a dovetail saw. Cut on the waste side of the lines, as you did when making the dovetails. Remove the waste with a chisel, then dry assemble the box to check the fit of the divider and guides in the notch. If the fit is too tight, shave the mitered surfaces with a chisel as necessary.

6

Round over the ends and edges of the bottom. The ends and edges of the bottom are rounded slightly. The radius of this round-over is too small to cut with a power tool. Instead, you'll find it easier to do by hand. First, "break" the top corners with a block plane, shaving the ends and edges round with repeated strokes. After you've roughed out the round-overs with a plane, sand or scrape them smooth. (See Figure 9.)

9/Round over the ends and edges of the bottom with a block plane, shaving the top corners. A "low-angle" block plane works best, particularly on the end grain.

7

Assemble the knife box. Finish sand all the parts, being careful not to round over any adjoining surfaces. Glue the guides to both sides of the divider. Let the glue set, then assemble the front, back, sides, and divider with glue. Reinforce the glue joint between the front, back, and divider with wire brads, and set the heads. When the glue dries, sand the dovetailed corners of the assembly clean.

Attach the bottom to the box assembly with wire brads. Do *not* glue the bottom to the box. The bottom must be free to expand and contract with changes in temperature and humidity. The brads will flex slightly to allow this movement, but glue would restrict it, causing the box to warp and the bottom to split.

Glue the pulls to the front ends of the lids. When the glue dries, fit the lids to the grooves in the back, sides, and guides. Using a scraper or fine sandpaper, remove small amounts of stock from the bottom surfaces of the lids until they slide in and out of the box assembly

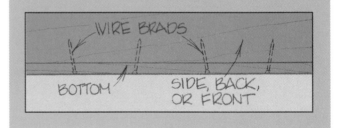

TRY THIS! To make sure the bottom stays firmly in place, drive the brads at slight angles. Vary the angle with each brad, so they hook the bottom to the box.

WIRE BRADS

BOTTOM

SIDE, BACK, OR FRONT

smoothly. When the lids are completely closed, the mitered ends of the pulls must fit flush against the mitered surfaces of the sides and guides.

8

Finish the knife box. Do any necessary touch-up sanding, and lightly break all the hard corners with sandpaper. If you wish, round them over to simulate years of wear and tear. Cover the heads of the brads with putty or stick shellac.

When the surface is properly prepared, apply a finish. Use a *penetrating* finish, such as tung oil or Danish oil — these won't build up in the grooves and cause the lids to stick. Carefully coat all wooden surfaces evenly, inside and out. This will help keep the parts from warping or cupping.

When the finish dries, buff it with wax. Lightly rub beeswax or paraffin on the edges of the lids to help them slide smoothly.

Wooden Briefcase

In his book, *Dress for Success,* John T. Molloy offers this advice about briefcases and attachés: "Attaché cases are always positive symbols of success, regardless of what they carry, and a lot more of them than you think are used only to carry lunch." The point is, an elegant briefcase or attaché makes a good impression, no matter what you use it for. And what could make a better impression than a finely crafted case made from rich hardwoods?

This briefcase is made of solid walnut and lined with hand-stitched leather. But despite its sophisticated looks, it's actually a very simple project. The case itself is nothing more than a wooden box with a handle, and the leatherwork requires only basic sewing skills. The elegance comes from the care with which you make the project.

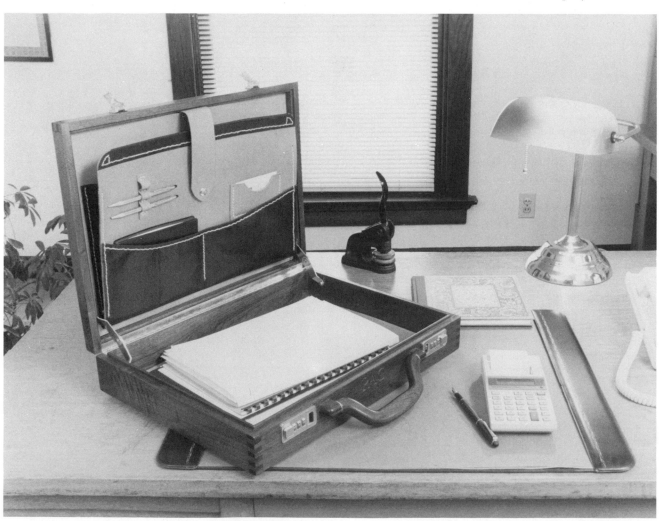

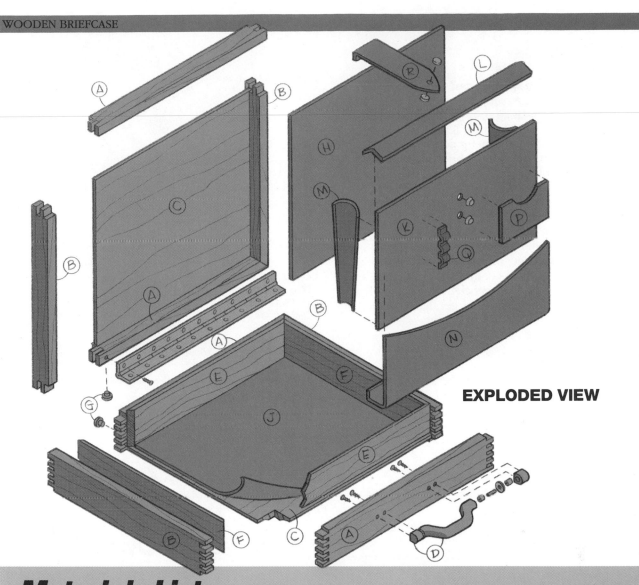

EXPLODED VIEW

Materials List

FINISHED DIMENSIONS

WOODEN PARTS

A. Front/back* (2) $\frac{1}{2}$" x $3\frac{1}{2}$"* x $18\frac{1}{4}$"

B. Sides* (2) $\frac{1}{2}$" x $3\frac{1}{2}$"* x $13\frac{1}{2}$"

C. Panels (2) $\frac{1}{4}$" x $12\frac{7}{8}$" x $17\frac{11}{16}$"

D. Handle** $\frac{3}{4}$" x $2\frac{1}{2}$" x $10\frac{3}{8}$"

E. Front/back lips (2) $\frac{1}{8}$" x $2\frac{3}{8}$" x $17\frac{1}{4}$"

F. Side lips (2) $\frac{1}{8}$" x $2\frac{3}{8}$" x $12\frac{1}{2}$"

G. Feet (4) $\frac{1}{2}$" dia. x $\frac{3}{8}$"

*Rip these parts after assembly to separate the lid from the case.
**Make this part from laminated hardwood.

LEATHER PARTS

H. Top lining $\frac{3}{64}$" x $12\frac{1}{2}$" x $17\frac{1}{4}$"

J. Bottom lining $\frac{3}{64}$" x $12\frac{1}{4}$" x 17"

K. Portfolio $\frac{1}{16}$" x 10" x 16"

L. Portfolio trim $\frac{3}{64}$" x 2" x 16"

M. Gussets (2) $\frac{3}{64}$" x 3" x 8"

N. Front pocket $\frac{3}{64}$" x 7" x 16"

P. Card pocket $\frac{1}{16}$" x $2\frac{1}{2}$" x $4\frac{3}{8}$"

Q. Pen holder $\frac{1}{16}$" x $\frac{3}{4}$" x $4\frac{1}{2}$"

R. Strap $\frac{1}{16}$" x $1\frac{3}{4}$" x $6\frac{1}{2}$"

HARDWARE

$\frac{1}{4}$" I.D. x $\frac{3}{8}$" O.D. x $\frac{3}{8}$" Bronze bushings (2)

$\frac{1}{4}$" dia. x $\frac{3}{4}$" Steel pins (2)

$\frac{1}{4}$" I.D. x $\frac{3}{4}$" O.D. Brass flat washers (2)

#4 x 1" Flathead wood screws (4)

1" x $17\frac{1}{4}$" Piano hinge and mounting screws

Lid support and mounting screws

Latches/locks and mounting screws (2)

Dowel buttons (4)

$\frac{3}{8}$" Brass brads (3)

Male snaps (2)

Female snap

Waxed string (50')

1

Select the stock and cut the parts to size. To make this project, you need about 6 board feet of 4/4 (four-quarters) stock, 5 square feet of thin, flexible leather, and 2 square feet of thicker, stiff leather. You can use any cabinet-grade wood, but the harder the wood is, the better the briefcase will wear. The case shown is made from walnut. Cherry, maple, oak, and teak also wear well.

Once you have selected the stock, plane 2½ board feet to ½″ thick and cut the front, back, and sides to size. Make *two* extra sides to use as test pieces. Resaw the remaining wood in half and plane it to ¼″ thick. Glue boards edge to edge to make the wide stock needed for the panels, and cut the panels to size. Then plane the remaining ¼″-thick stock to ⅛″. Rip the lips to width, but cut them about 1″ longer than specified in the Materials List. Laminate the rest of the ⅛″-thick stock to make ¾″-thick hardwood plywood for the handle. (See Figure 1.)

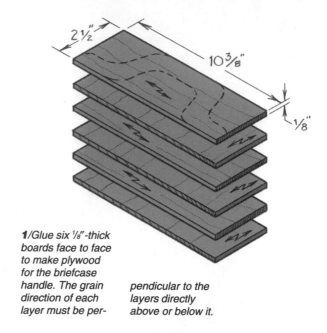

1/Glue six ⅛″-thick boards face to face to make plywood for the briefcase handle. The grain direction of each layer must be per- pendicular to the layers directly above or below it.

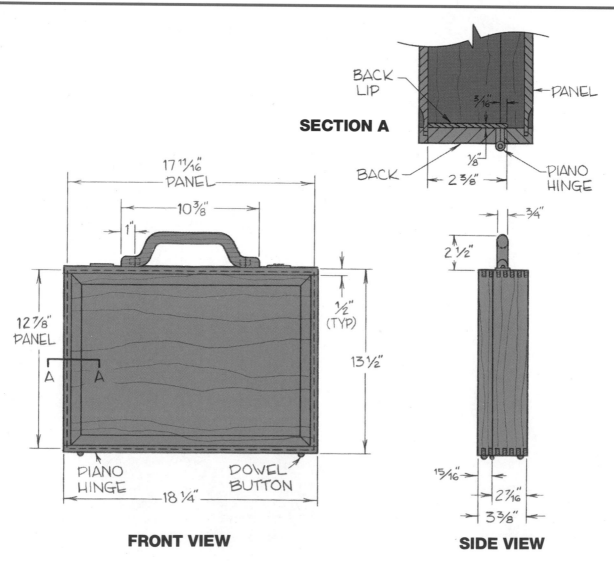

SECTION A

BACK LIP

PANEL

³⁄₁₆″

BACK

⅛″

2 ³⁄₈″

PIANO HINGE

17 ¹¹⁄₁₆″ PANEL

10 ³⁄₈″

1″

12 ⁷⁄₈″ PANEL

A   A

½″ (TYP)

13 ½″

PIANO HINGE

DOWEL BUTTON

18 ¼″

FRONT VIEW

¾″

2 ½″

¹⁵⁄₁₆″

2 ⁷⁄₁₆″

3 ³⁄₈″

SIDE VIEW

2

Cut finger joints in the front, back, and sides. The front, back, and sides of the brief-case are joined with ¼"-wide box joints, or finger joints. There are several ways to cut these joints, but one of the easiest is to use a simple jig that mounts to the miter gauge of a table saw or table-mounted router. Refer to Step-by-Step: Making Finger Joints for complete instructions.

Note: Cut finger joints in the test pieces before cutting good stock.

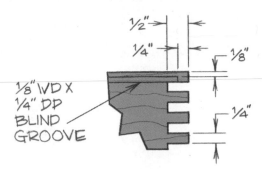

⅛" WD X ¼" DP BLIND GROOVE

FINGER JOINT LAYOUT

Step-by-Step: Making Finger Joints

Finger joints, or box joints as they're sometimes called, are sets of interlocking tenons or "fingers" used to join the corners of wooden boxes, cases, and drawers. These multiple fingers increase the gluing surface at each corner, strengthening the joint.

You can make finger joints with either a table saw or a table-mounted router; however, you'll need to make a jig to attach to your miter gauge. The *Finger Joint Jig* shown can be adapted to fit most equipment.

Attach the jig to the miter gauge, centering the bolts in the slot. (You should have room to slide the jig *at least* ¾" right or left. If you're using a table

saw, mount a dado cutter on the arbor. If you're using a table-mounted router, secure a straight bit in the collet. The cutter or the bit should be the same width as the fingers you want to make. Cut a slot in the bottom edge of the jig, as shown in the drawing. Make a 4"-long stick *precisely* the same width as the cutter or bit. Cut this tenon in two parts, one approximately 1½" long and the other 2½" long. Glue the shorter piece in the slot in the jig. This will serve as a stop to space the fingers evenly. Keep the other piece to use as a gauge to help position the jig.

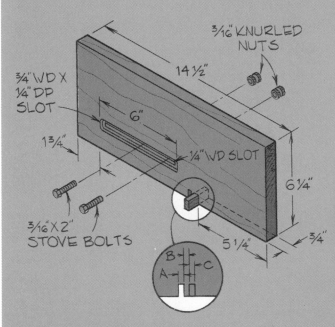

¾" WD X ¼" DP SLOT

3/16" KNURLED NUTS

14½"

6"

1¾"

¼" WD SLOT

3/16" X 2" STOVE BOLTS

5¼"

6¼"

¾"

FINGER JOINT JIG

NOTE: Measurements A, B, and C must all be equal.

1

To use the jig, *first adjust the position of the jig on the miter gauge. Slide it sideways so the distance between the stop and the cutter or bit is **precisely** the same as the width of the stop. Use the wooden gauge you made to measure this distance. Turn on the saw or router and cut another slot, as shown in the drawing.*

(Continued)

Step-by-Step: Making Finger Joints — Continued

2

Mark the top edges of the two boards you wish to join. Scribe the baselines of the fingers on **both** the inside and outside surfaces — this will keep the stock from chipping or tearing as you pass it over the cutter or bit.

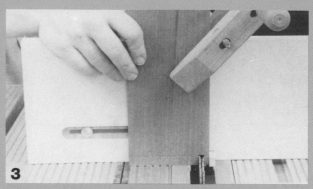

3

Place the first board against the jig with the top edge resting on the table. Slide it sideways until the **top** edge butts against the jig stop. Clamp the board to the jig. Turn on the saw or router and cut a slot, pushing the miter gauge forward and retracting it. This will create a single finger.

4

Lift the board and slide it over, fitting the slot over the stop. Make another cut, then repeat this procedure until you've cut the first set of fingers.

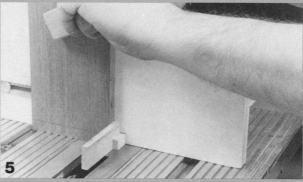

5

To cut a mating set of fingers in the second board, use the gauge as a spacer. Insert it between the jig stop and the cutter or bit. Butt the top edge of the second board against the gauge, clamp it in place, and make a cut — the dado cutter or router bit will create a notch in the top corner of the board.

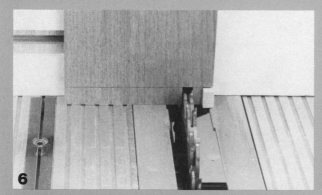

6

Remove the gauge and set it aside. Slide the second board sideways on the jig until the notch fits over the stop. Cut the remaining fingers in the second board following the same procedure used for the first.

7

Fit the fingers together. Both the top and bottom edges of the two boards should be flush. The interlocking fingers should be snug, but not overly so. If they're too tight, the stop is too far away from the cutter or bit. If they're loose, it's too close. If necessary, readjust the position of the jig on the miter gauge and try again.

3

Cut the grooves in the front, back, and sides. The panels rest in ⅛″-wide, ¼″-deep grooves in the front, back, and sides. These grooves are double-blind — they stop ¼″ from each end of each piece so they won't show on the outside of the completed case.

Rout these grooves with a table-mounted router and a ⅛″ straight bit. Use a fence to guide the work. Before you begin the cuts, stick a piece of masking tape to the fence behind the bit. Using a square, mark the left and right sides (the diameter) of the bit on the tape, ½″

above the work surface. Also, lay out the grooves on the *outside* faces of the boards — opposite the faces you will actually cut. (See Figure 2.)

To make each groove, slowly lower the board onto the bit, keeping the edge pressed against the fence. Move the board to the right until the left-hand mark on the fence lines up with the layout line that indicates the left end of the groove. (See Figure 3.) Move the board back toward the right and line up the two right-hand marks. While you work, keep the edge of the board against the fence.

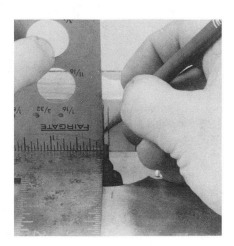

2/To rout a blind groove on a router table, you must know where to start and stop cutting. Since neither the bit nor the cut will be visible as you work, mark the diameter of the bit on the fence. Lay out the grooves on the opposite side of the board from the one you want to cut.

3/As you cut the groove, stop when the layout line that indicates the blind end of the groove lines up with the appropriate mark on the fence.

4

Make the raised panels. On the briefcase shown, the panels are raised, as shown in the *Raised Panel Detail*. However, you can make flush panels instead, as shown in the *Flush Panel Detail*.

Note: If you elect to make flush panels, use plywood instead of solid wood — it's more stable. Solid wood will expand and contract, creating noticeable cracks between the panels and the other parts.

To make a flush panel, simply cut a ¼″-wide, ⅛″-deep dado all the way around the perimeter. To make a raised panel, cut a ½″-wide, ⅛″-deep rabbet, then rout a cove in the rabbet shoulders with a core-box bit. (See Figure 4.)

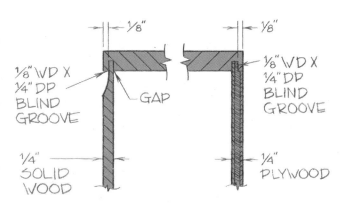

RAISED PANEL DETAIL   FLUSH PANEL DETAIL

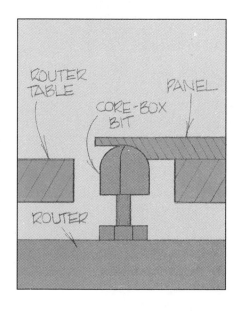

4/To make the raised panels, first rabbet the ends and edges to fit the grooves in the front, back, and sides. Then round the shoulders of these rabbets with a table-mounted router and a core-box bit.

5 Assemble the case and cut the lid.

Finish sand the parts you've made so far —
front, back, sides, and panels. Test assemble them to
check the fit of the joints, then assemble the front, back,
and sides with glue. Put the panels in place as you
assemble the other parts, but do *not* glue them in their
grooves. Let them "float," so they can expand and contract with changes in humidity.

Let the glue dry for at least 24 hours, then sand the
finger joints clean and flush. Rip the lid from the case
on a table saw, cutting the front and back first, then the
sides. When you cut the last side, put several wedges in
the kerfs to hold them open. Clamp parts together to
pinch the wedges in place. (See Figure 5.) If you don't
use these wedges, the kerfs will close as you make the
final cut, the saw will bind, and the mating edges of the
lid and case will be uneven.

Note: When you rip the lid from the case, don't
"split a finger." Position the kerf so it falls *between* two
fingers, shaving a little stock from both. If you have a
thin-kerf blade, use it.

5/When ripping the lid from the assembled case, use wedges to keep the kerfs from closing as you make the final cut. Hold the wedges in place by pinching them in the kerfs with clamps.

6 Hinge the lid to the case.

The lid is held
to the case with a long piano hinge. Mortise the
case back and lid back, then install the hinge. Make
sure that the edges of the hinge are flush with the inside
surfaces of the back parts. Also check that when the lid
is closed, all the outside surfaces are flush.

7 Install the feet.

To keep the back of the brief-
case off the floor when you set it down, the case
rests on four "feet". These feet are actually ½" wooden
screw hole buttons, which you can purchase from most
woodworking suppliers. Drill ½"-diameter, ¼"-deep
holes in the back near each corner, then glue the buttons in the holes. (See Figure 6.)

6/Install ½" screw hole buttons on the back of the case to serve as feet. These are available in several different species of hardwoods.

8 Install the locks and latches.

On the
case shown, the lid is held closed by combination locks. These are available from several mail-order
woodworking supply companies. Here are two:

The Woodworkers' Store
21801 Industrial Blvd.
Rogers, MN 55374-9514

Woodworker's Supply
5604 Alameda Place
Albuquerque, NM 87113

The combination locks must be mortised into the front
of the case. Carefully lay out the position of the locks
and latches, then rout the mortises. (The size and depth
of these mortises will vary with the make of the locks.
Carefully measure the hardware before routing.)

Test fit the locks in the mortises. If they fit properly,
install the locks and latches with screws.

9 Make and install the handle.

Enlarge the *Handle Pattern* and trace it onto the stock. Cut the shape with a band saw or scroll saw and sand the sawed edges.

Round over the edges of the handle that are shaded on the pattern, using a 3/8″ quarter-round bit and a table-mounted router. Do *not* round over the edges where the handle mounts will attach to the case.

Cut the handle mounts from the handle. Bore 3/8″-diameter, 3/8″-deep holes in the cut ends of the mounts. Insert dowel centers in these holes, then press them against the cut ends of the handle. Bore matching holes where the dowel centers leave indentations. In each of these holes, glue a 1/4″-I.D, 3/8″-O.D. bushing with epoxy. File the ends of the bushings so they are flush with the cut ends of the handle and mounts.

Insert the steel pins in the mount bushings; place the brass washers over the pins; then insert the other ends of the pins in the handle. Clamp the mounts to the front of the case and test the action of the handle. It should pivot a full 180°. If it binds at any point, carefully file stock from the handle. When it pivots properly, attach the mounts to the front with flathead wood screws. Do *not* glue the mounts in place at this time.

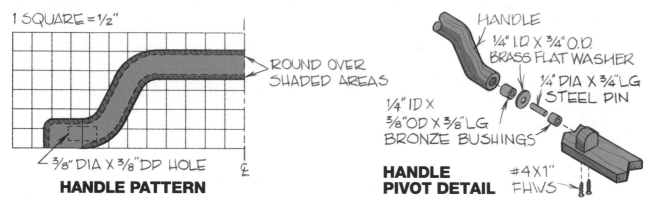

1 SQUARE = 1/2″

ROUND OVER SHADED AREAS

3/8″ DIA X 3/8″ DP HOLE

HANDLE PATTERN

HANDLE

1/4″ I.D. X 3/4″ O.D. BRASS FLAT WASHER

1/4″ DIA X 3/4″ LG STEEL PIN

1/4″ ID X 3/8″ OD X 3/8″ LG BRONZE BUSHINGS

#4 X 1″ FHWS

HANDLE PIVOT DETAIL

10 Make and fit the lips.

The inside of the case is lined with 1/8″-thick lips. These lips keep the lid square on the case, and hide the handle screws and the lock mortises. Round over the top edge of the lips with a file and sandpaper. Then miter the ends of the lips to fit snugly inside the case. Slide the lips into position, but do *not* glue them to the case yet. Attach a lid support to one side of the case and lid. Test the action of the lid — it should open and close easily without binding on the lips.

11 Assemble and finish the briefcase.

When you've fitted all the wooden parts, remove the lips, handle, and hardware. Finish sand all the parts that still need it. Attach the handle to the case with glue and screws. Then glue the lips to the inside surfaces of the front, back, and sides.

Do any necessary touch-up sanding, then apply a finish to all wooden surfaces. Choose a hard, water-resistant finish that's easy to repair, such as tung oil or urethane oil. Apply several coats, covering the inside and outside of the case evenly. Let the finish dry completely and rub it out. Do *not* wax it or buff it yet.

12 Make the portfolio.

Like most briefcases, this one has a leather portfolio in the lid to hold loose papers. Making this portfolio requires a few simple leatherworking tools — a punch to make holes for the stitches, a star wheel to accurately space the stitches, two needles to do the stitching, and a setter and anvil to install the snaps. (See Figure 7.) You can purchase these at all leathercraft stores and many hobby stores.

Cut the leather parts to the sizes specified in the Materials List. On the project shown, the portfolio, card pocket, pen holder, and strap are all cut from stiff cowhide. The other parts are made from a flexible pigskin.

Enlarge the *Front Pocket Pattern, Card Pocket Pattern,* and *Strap Pattern*. Trace these onto the leather parts. Also lay out the shapes of the gussets and portfolio trim. Cut the shapes with a razor-sharp knife.

All the parts are stitched together using the same technique. First, glue the parts together with rubber cement. With a star wheel, trace where you want to put the stitches. (See Figure 8.) The wheel leaves tiny, evenly spaced indentations to show where each stitch begins and ends. Punch a hole at each indentation. (See Figure 9.)

Cut a length of waxed string and thread a needle on each end. Push one needle through the first hole and pull the string halfway through. Then push one needle

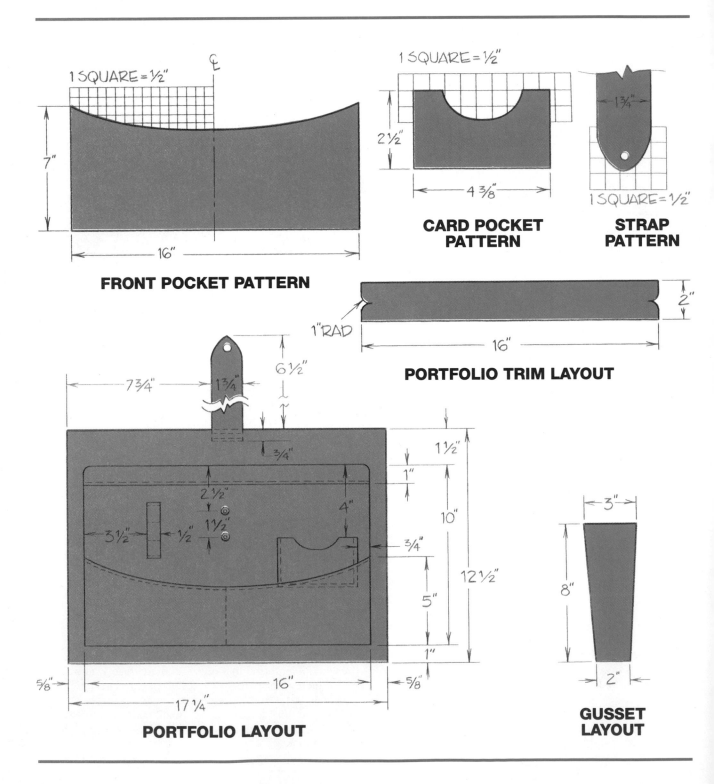

FRONT POCKET PATTERN

CARD POCKET PATTERN

STRAP PATTERN

PORTFOLIO TRIM LAYOUT

PORTFOLIO LAYOUT

GUSSET LAYOUT

down through the second hole, and the other needle up through the same hole. Repeat for each hole, making a simple "over-and-under" stitch. (See Figure 10.)

The leather parts must be stitched together in the proper order. First, attach the portfolio trim, card pocket, and pen holder to the portfolio. (See Figure 11.) Also install two male snaps near the center of the portfolio. You'll use the bottom snap when the portfolio is empty, and the top snap when it's full.

"Double" the top edge of the front pocket, and both the top and bottom edges of the gussets, folding over about ¼″ of material. Stitch the doubled edges. Then sew the pocket and the gussets to the portfolio. (See Figure 12.) These parts must be sewn together all at once in three layers. Don't try to sew the gusset first, then the pocket — or the other way around. The stitches will look messy.

When the portfolio is completely assembled, sew the back edges of the front pocket and the gussets to the top liner. Attach a female snap near the end of the strap, and sew the strap to the liner as well. (See Figure 13.)

7/To make the leather portfolio, you need a few basic leatherworking tools (clockwise from the top): a hole punch, a star wheel, a snap setter and anvil, and two needles.

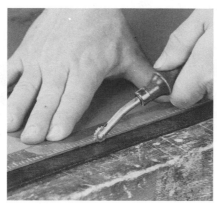

8/To evenly space the stitches, mark their location with a star wheel. Press hard, so the wheel leaves indentations on the leather.

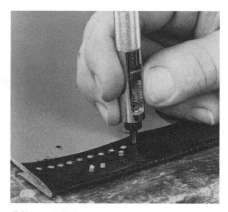

9/At each indentation left by the star wheel, punch a small hole. Back up the leather with a scrap of softwood.

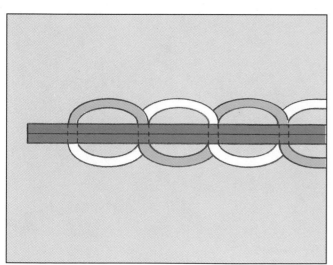

10/With two needles and one length of string, sew the leather parts together with an "over-and-under" stitch, as shown.

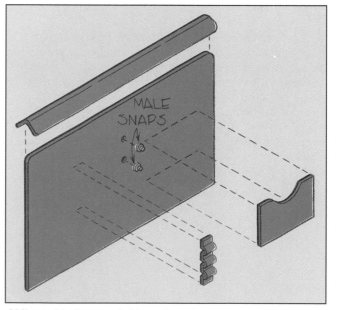

MALE SNAPS

11/Assemble the leather parts in the proper order. First, sew the trim, card pocket, and pen holder to the portfolio. Also install the male snaps.

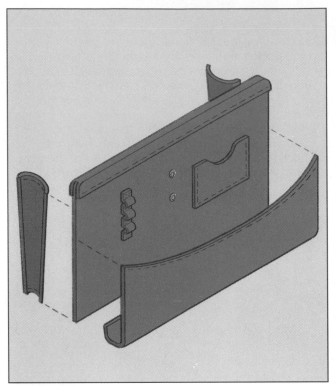

12/Next, attach the front pocket and gussets. Sew all these parts together at once, in three layers.

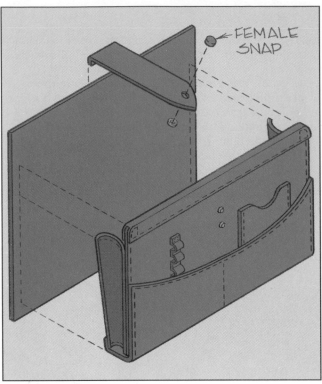

FEMALE SNAP

13/Finally, sew the gussets, front pocket, and strap to the top liner. Install a female snap near the end of the strap.

13

Install the leatherwork in the briefcase. Glue both the top and bottom liners to the inside surfaces of the panels, using contact cement. Make sure the edges of the top liner butt up against the front, back, and sides of the lid. The bottom liner must butt against the lips. Keep the strap from pulling out by driving several small brass brads through the strap and into the front of the lid. (See Figure 14.)

Wax and buff all the wooden surfaces, and clean and oil the leatherwork.

14/Reinforce the strap by tacking it to the front of the lid. If you don't tack it in place, it may pull the top liner loose.

Closet Organizer

The average closet is a monument to disorganization. There's no fixed system, no logical order. Most of us hang up our clothes wherever there's an empty space, then sort through the jumble until we uncover what we're after.

The problem seems to be that traditional closets aren't always designed for what people keep in them. Consider that most of the clothes you hang up in closets (shirts, skirts, pants, sweaters) take up less than 36″ of vertical space, yet closets usually offer 66″. A few items (long coats and dresses) require a longer space, but not the majority. Many clothes are best stored on shelves (shoes, hats, sweaters, and linens), yet most closets have only a single, hard-to-reach shelf above the hanger rod. As a result, certain areas are overcrowded, others are largely vacant, and the closet seems disorganized.

This simple system of rods and shelves does a better job of organizing the clothes. The two long rods are 38″ and 76″ off the floor, furnishing plenty of hanging storage for short items. The shorter rod accommodates longer clothes. An adjustable shelving unit separates the two hanging storage areas and provides lots of accessible shelves. *All* the closet space is used efficiently, and the clothes are easier to find and reach. ●

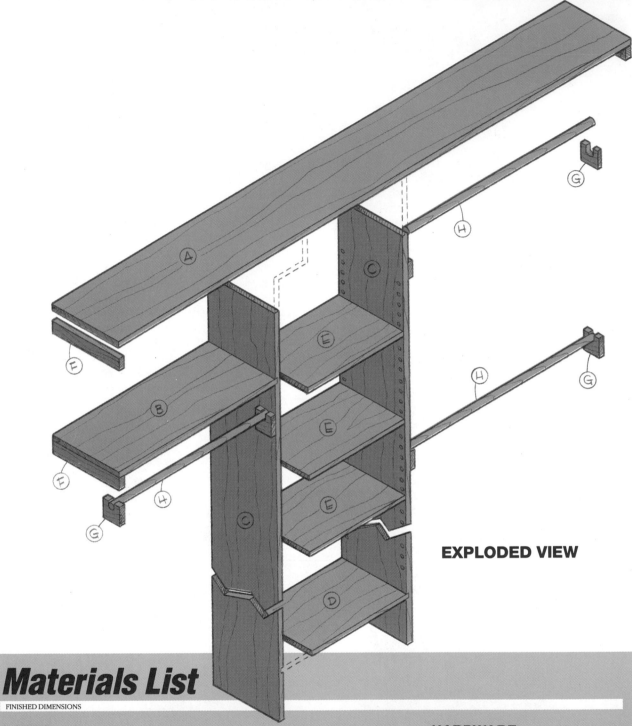

EXPLODED VIEW

Materials List

FINISHED DIMENSIONS

PARTS

A. Long upper shelf $3/4''$ x $14''$ x (variable)

B. Short upper shelf $3/4''$ x $14''$ x (variable)

C. Shelving supports (2) $3/4''$ x $14''$ x $79 5/8''$

D. Fixed shelf $3/4''$ x $14''$ x (variable)

E. Adjustable shelves (1–6) $3/4''$ x $14''$ x (variable)

F. Cleats (2–3) $3/4''$ x $1 1/2''$ x $14''$

G. Hanger rod brackets (2–6) $3/4''$ x $3''$ x $4''$

H. Hanger rods (1–3) $1 1/4''$ dia. x (variable)

HARDWARE

#10 x $1 1/4''$ Flathead wood screws (12–24)

#12 x $2 1/2''$ Flathead wood screws (2–8)

Molly anchors (2–6)

L-brackets and mounting screws (2–4)

Shelving support pins (4 per adjustable shelf)

1

Lay out the shelves and hanger rods.
Measure the inside of your closet and make a sketch of it *without* any of the existing shelves or hanger rods. On this sketch, draw a single shelf, 80″ above the floor, running the length of your closet. (This is probably 10″–12″ above your present closet shelf.) Next, draw a simple vertical shelving unit under the long shelf, dividing the closet into two sections — one on either side of the shelving unit. Unless you have a lot of full-length coats or dresses to store, don't put this unit in the middle of the closet. Offset it 1′–2′ to one side or the other. This will give you more hanging space for ordinary (short) clothes.

In the larger of the two sections, draw two hanger rods 38″ and 76″ off the floor. These will hold the short clothes — pants, shirts, etc. In the smaller section, draw a single rod 64″ off the floor for longer items. If you wish, add another shelf just above this rod.

When you've finished, your sketch will look something like the *Sample Layout*. Use this plan to figure the amount of materials you need, cut the parts to size, and make the joinery.

2

Select the stock and cut the parts to size. You can make the shelves, shelving supports, cleats, and hanger rod brackets from ³⁄₄″ pine shelving stock, plywood, or particleboard. (The unit shown is made from plywood and faced with strips of pine to hide the plies.) Make the hanger rods from 1¼″-diameter closet poles. When you have selected and purchased the materials, cut the parts to size. If necessary, face the front edges of any plywood parts.

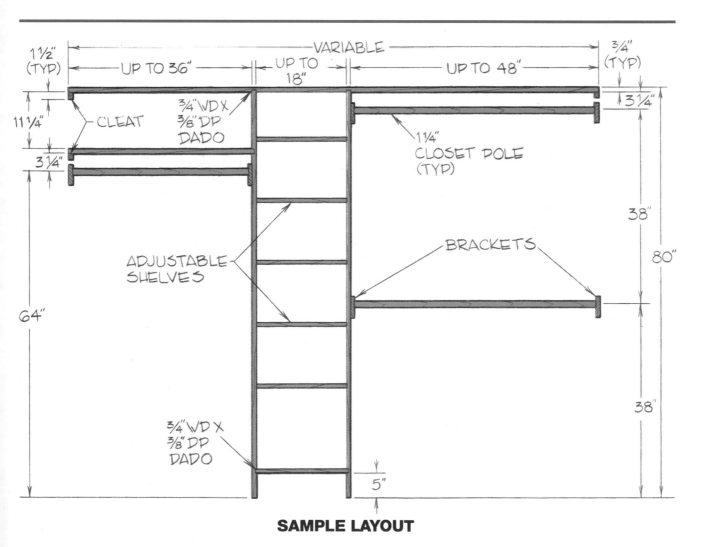

SAMPLE LAYOUT

3

Cut the joinery in the upper shelf and shelving supports. The top ends of the shelving supports fit into two ³/₄″-wide, ³/₈″-deep dadoes in the long upper shelf. The fixed shelf and the short upper shelf (if you've added one) rest in dadoes in the shelving supports. Cut the dadoes with a dado cutter or hand-held router.

4

Drill the holes in the shelving supports. The adjustable shelves rest on movable, pin-style supports. These pins fit in ¼″-diameter, ³/₈″-deep holes in the shelving supports. Lay out the locations of the holes on the supports, as shown in the *Shelving Support Layout*. Then drill them with a portable power drill. Use a stop collar to ensure that the holes will be the proper depth.

5

Cut the hanger rod brackets. The hanger rods rest in brackets that are open on the top end. This lets you easily install and remove the hanger rods. To make a bracket, drill a 1³/₈″-diameter hole through the stock. Then open up the top side of the hole with a band saw or hand saw. (See Figure 1.)

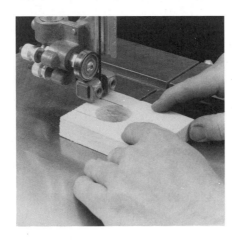

1/To make a hanger rod bracket, first drill a hole through the wood. Cut through to the hole from the top edge, removing stock and opening up the hole.

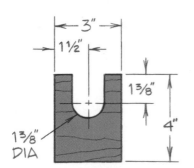

HANGER ROD BRACKET LAYOUT

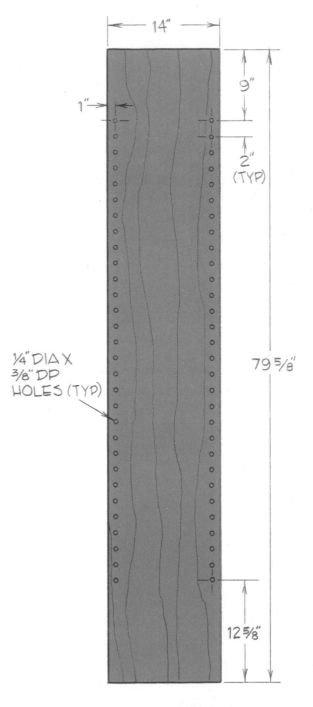

¼″ DIA X ³/₈″ DP HOLES (TYP)

SHELVING SUPPORT LAYOUT

6 Install the shelves in the closet.

Remove the doors and clothes from the closet, and discard the old shelf and hanger rod. Locate the studs in the side and back walls. Attach cleats to the side wall with #12 x 2½" flathead wood screws, driving the screws through the cleats and into the studs. Countersink the heads of the screws. (If you're mounting the cleats on masonry, install expandable lead anchors in the walls, then attach the cleats to the anchors with lag screws.)

Glue the fixed shelf between the shelving supports, and reinforce the joint with #10 x 1¼" flathead wood screws. Have a helper hold the supports upright in the closet. Apply glue to one end of the short upper shelf. Fit this to the dado in one of the supports, and reinforce with screws. Then attach the other end of the shelf to a cleat with screws.

Apply glue to the top ends of the supports. Lay the long upper shelf across them, fitting the ends into the dadoes. Reinforce with screws, and use screws to attach the ends of the upper shelf to the cleats.

Using a plumb bob or a level, check that the shelving supports are plumb. If they're not, tap the bottom ends to one side as necessary. Then fasten the back edges to

2/Fasten the shelving supports to the back closet wall with L-brackets.

the wall with L-brackets. (See Figure 2.) Use screws to attach the L-brackets to the supports. Also use screws to attach the brackets wherever they are positioned over wall studs. Where they aren't positioned over a stud, use Molly anchors to fasten them to the wall.

7 Install the hanger rods.

Measure and mark the positions of the hanger rod brackets. Remember, no matter what the height, the front edges of the brackets should be flush with the front edges of the shelving supports. Secure the brackets that attach to the shelving supports with glue and screws. Secure those brackets that fasten to the walls with screws (where they're positioned over a stud) or Molly anchors (where they aren't). When the glue dries, drop the hanger rods into the brackets. (See Figure 3.)

3/The hanger rods drop into their brackets from above — and come out the same way.

8 Finish the shelves and rods.

If you wish, paint the shelves and rods to match the inside of the closet. Use a washable, high-gloss paint — it's easier to keep clean than flat or satin finishes. When the paint dries, install the doors and put the clothes back in your closet.

TRY THIS! Always paint the insides of your closets white or a pastel color. This reflects the light and makes it easier to find items stored there.

Built-In Utility Cupboards

Need extra storage space in your laundry room, garage, or workshop, but don't want to spend a lot of time or money? This cupboard system may be what you're looking for — it's fairly inexpensive, easy to build, and simple to install. The system consists of three different modules — countertop cupboard, wall cupboard, and standing cupboard. You can arrange these modules or adjust their sizes to fit almost any space.

These cupboards were built by Larry Callahan of West Milton, Ohio. His design is extremely simple — each cupboard is a large plywood box with doors. Inside each box are shelves, drawers, and/or bins. There are no complex interior assemblies; instead, the shelves rest in simple dadoes, and the drawers and bins are mounted on extension slides. All three units are attached to the wall by cleats, using screws or bolts.

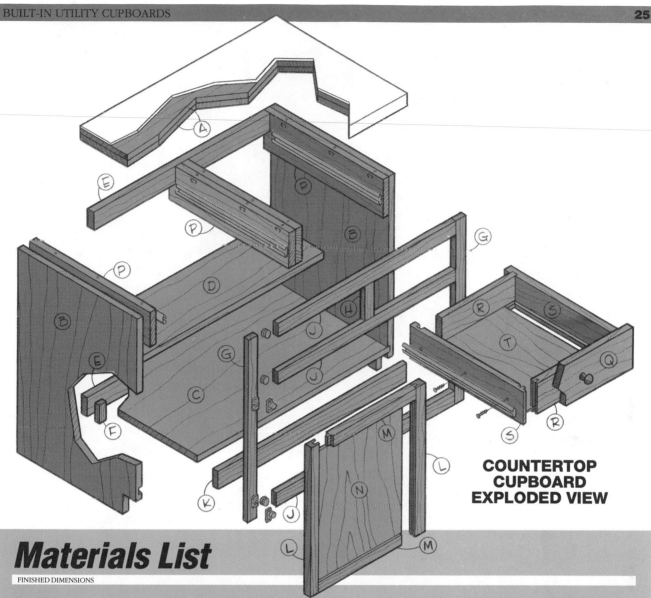

COUNTERTOP
CUPBOARD
EXPLODED VIEW

Materials List

FINISHED DIMENSIONS

PARTS

Countertop Cupboard

A. Countertop
   layers* (2)   ³/₄" x 24" x 35"

B. Sides* (2)   ³/₄" x 21¼" x 34"

C. Shelf*   ³/₄" x 21¼" x 34¼"

D. Half-shelf*   ³/₄" x 10" x 34¼"

E. Cleats (3)   ³/₄" x 2" x 33½"

F. Nailing
   blocks (4)   ³/₄" x ³/₄" x 2"

G. Face frame outside
   stiles (2)   ³/₄" x 1½" x 31"

H. Face frame
   inside stile   ³/₄" x 1½" x 4"

J. Face frame
   rails (3)   ³/₄" x 1½" x 32"

K. Toeboard   ³/₄" x 3" x 35"

L. Door stiles (4)   ³/₄" x 1³/₄" x 23³/₄"

M. Door rails (4)   ³/₄" x 1³/₄" x 14³/₄"

N. Door
   panels* (2)   ¼" x 14⁵/₈" x 21⅛"

P. Drawer mount
   spacers (4)   ³/₄" x 5½" x 21¼"

Q. Drawer
   faces (2)   ³/₄" x 5¼" x 17⅛"

R. Drawer fronts/
   backs (4)   ³/₄" x 4" x 13½"

S. Drawer sides (4)   ³/₄" x 4" x 20¼"

T. Drawer
   bottoms* (2)   ¼" x 13½" x 19"

Make these parts from plywood.

HARDWARE

Countertop Cupboard

4d Finishing nails (¼ lb.)

#10 x 1½" Flathead wood screws
   (24)

#10 Wooden plates (16)

European-style surface-mounted
   hinges and mounting screws (4)

20" Extension slides and mounting
   screws (4)

Plastic laminate (4' x 4' sheet)

¼" x 3" Lag screws (6)

Drawer/door pulls (4)

(Continued)

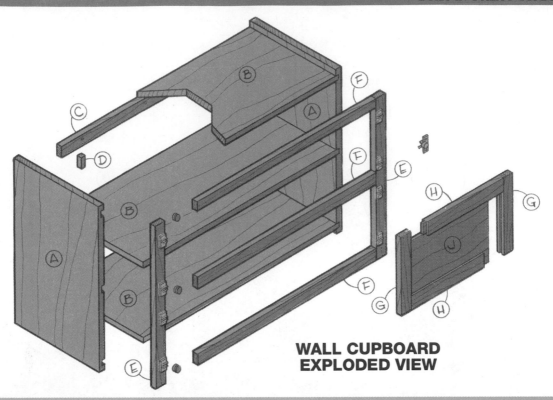

**WALL CUPBOARD
EXPLODED VIEW**

Materials List — *Continued*

FINISHED DIMENSIONS

PARTS

Wall Cupboard

A.	Sides* (2)	³/₄″ x 15¹/₄″ x 24³/₄″
B.	Shelves* (3)	³/₄″ x 15¹/₄″ x 34¹/₄″
C.	Cleats (2)	³/₄″ x 2″ x 33¹/₂″
D.	Nailing blocks (4)	³/₄″ x ³/₄″ x 2″
E.	Face frame stiles (2)	³/₄″ x 1¹/₂″ x 24³/₄″
F.	Face frame rails (3)	³/₄″ x 1¹/₂″ x 32″
G.	Door stiles (8)	³/₄″ x 1³/₄″ x 11³/₈″
H.	Door rails (8)	³/₄″ x 1³/₄″ x 14³/₄″
J.	Door panels* (4)	¹/₄″ x 8³/₄″ x 14⁵/₈″

Standing Cupboard

A.	Sides* (2)	³/₄″ x 21¹/₄″ x 82″
B.	Shelves* (3)	³/₄″ x 21¹/₄″ x 23¹/₄″
C.	Half-shelf*	³/₄″ x 10″ x 23¹/₄″
D.	Cleats (4)	³/₄″ x 2″ x 22¹/₂″
E.	Nailing blocks (8)	³/₄″ x ³/₄″ x 2″
F.	Face frame stiles (2)	³/₄″ x 1¹/₂″ x 79″

G.	Face frame rails (5)	³/₄″ x 1¹/₂″ x 21″
H.	Toeboard	³/₄″ x 3″ x 24″
J.	Door stiles (12)	³/₄″ x 1³/₄″ x 23³/₄″
K.	Door rails (12)	³/₄″ x 1³/₄″ x 9¹/₄″
L.	Door panels* (6)	¹/₄″ x 9¹/₈″ x 21¹/₈″
M.	Drawer mount spacers (10)	³/₄″ x 5¹/₂″ x 21¹/₄″
N.	Drawer face	³/₄″ x 5¹/₄″ x 23¹/₂″
P.	Drawer front/back (2)	³/₄″ x 4″ x 19¹/₄″
Q.	Drawer sides (2)	³/₄″ x 4″ x 20¹/₄″
R.	Drawer bottom*	¹/₄″ x 19″ x 19¹/₄″
S.	Bin sides (16)	³/₄″ x 3 x 20″
T.	Bin rails (16)	³/₄″ x ³/₄″ x 20″
U.	Bin dowels (144)	³/₈″ dia. x 6″
V.	Bin bottoms* (4)	¹/₄″ x 19¹/₄″ x 19¹/₄″

Make these parts from plywood.

HARDWARE

Wall Cupboard

4d Finishing nails (¹/₈ lb.)

#10 x 1¹/₂″ Flathead wood screws (18)

#10 Wooden plates (12)

European-style surface-mounted hinges and mounting screws (8)

¹/₄″ x 3″ Lag screws (4)

Door pulls (4)

Standing Cupboard

4d Finishing nails (¹/₄ lb.)

#10 x 1¹/₂″ Flathead wood screws (24)

#10 Wooden plates (20)

European-style surface-mounted hinges and mounting screws (12)

20″ Extension slides and mounting screws (10)

¹/₄″ x 3″ Lag screws (8)

Drawer/door pulls (8)

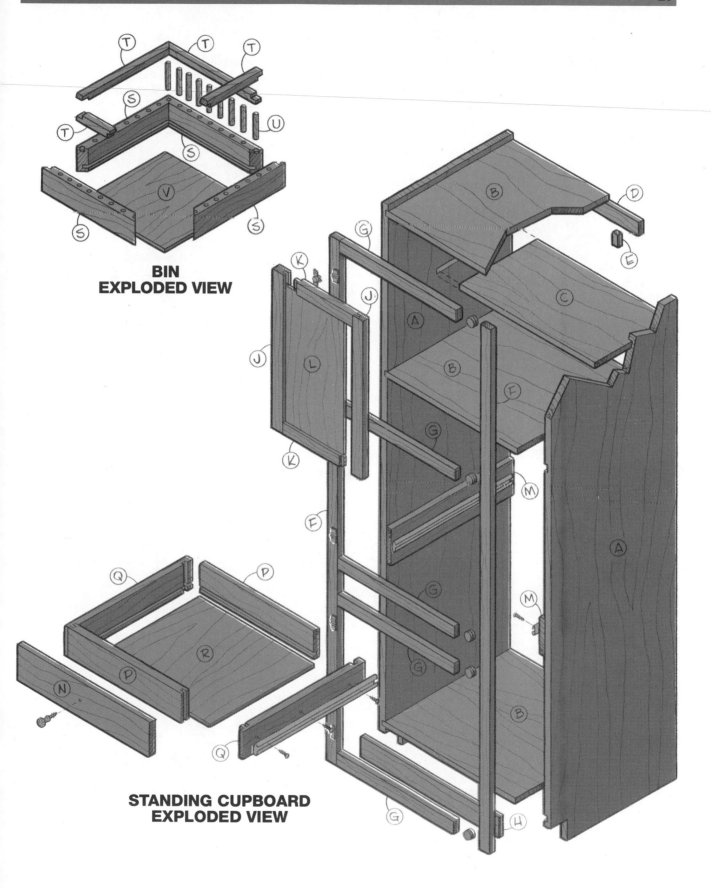

**BIN
EXPLODED VIEW**

**STANDING CUPBOARD
EXPLODED VIEW**

1

Determine the configuration and sizes of the cupboards. Measure the area where you want to install this project, then give some thought as to what kinds of cupboards you need, how many you need, and how you will arrange them. As you design your cupboard system, remember that you can change the sizes of these pieces if you need to. You can make them wider, narrower, taller, or shorter to fit a par-

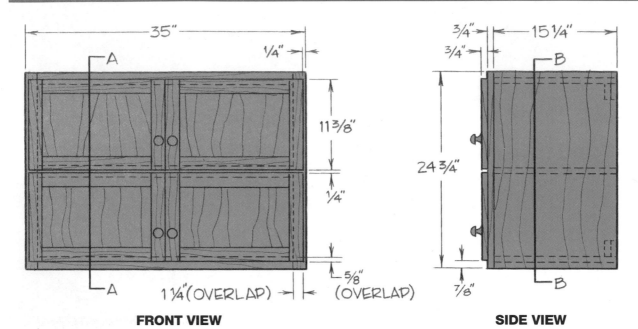

ticular space. You can also alter the arrangement of the shelves, half-shelves, drawers, and doors.

Sketch a front view of the cupboard system you wish to build, and calculate the materials you'll need. This sketch doesn't have to be as detailed as the drawings in this chapter, but it should provide adequate information to estimate the materials, cut the parts to size, and make the joinery.

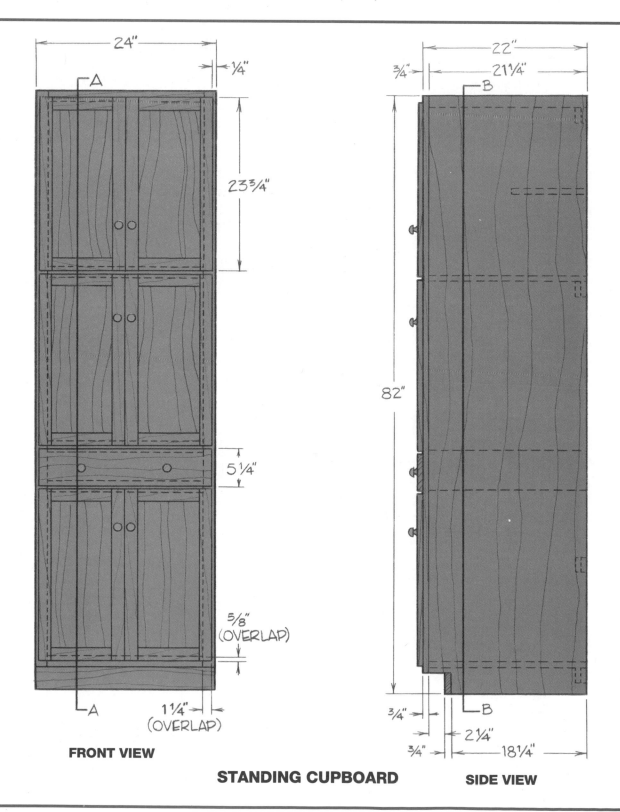

FRONT VIEW

STANDING CUPBOARD   **SIDE VIEW**

2 Select the stock and cut the parts to size.

Select the stock and cut the parts to size. As shown, each of the cupboard units requires a different amount of material:

- To build the *countertop cupboard,* you need one and one-half 4′ x 8′ sheets of ¾″ plywood, one 4′ x 4′ sheet of ¼″ plywood, and 16 board feet of 4/4 (four-quarters) stock.
- To build the *wall cupboard,* you need one 4′ x 8′ sheet of ¾″ plywood, one 4′ x 4′ sheet of ¼″ plywood, and 7 board feet of 4/4 stock.
- To build the *standing cupboard,* you need one and one-half 4′ x 8′ sheets of ¾″ plywood, one 4′ x 8′ sheet of ¼″ plywood, and 36 board feet of 4/4 stock.

If you've changed the dimensions of these units, they may require different amounts of materials.

You can build these cupboards from any cabinet-grade wood and plywood. If you plan to apply a stain or natural finish, the plywood veneer should match the solid stock. If you intend to paint the completed cupboard, it won't matter whether or not the plywood matches the stock — the grain will be hidden.

Once you have purchased the stock, plane the 4/4 stock to ¾″ thick. Cut all the case and face frame parts to size, carefully labeling them so you know what part goes with what unit. Do *not* cut the door, drawer, or bin parts to size yet; wait until after you've assembled and installed the cases.

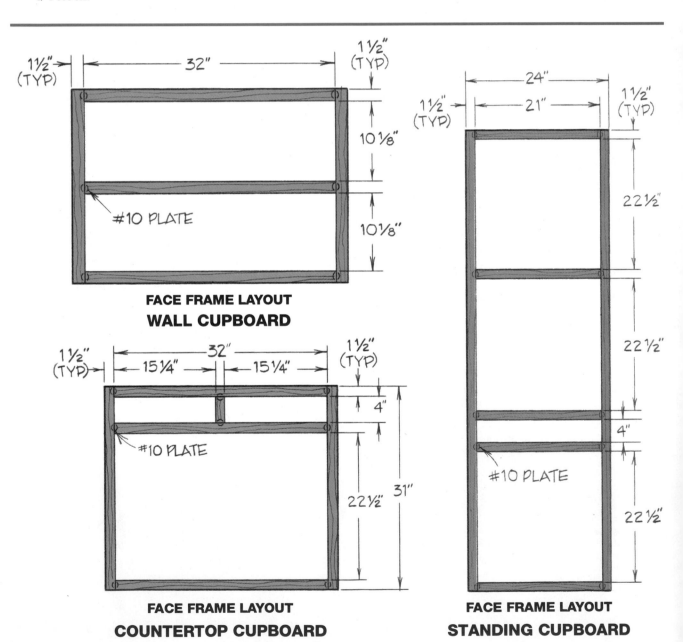

FACE FRAME LAYOUT
WALL CUPBOARD

FACE FRAME LAYOUT
COUNTERTOP CUPBOARD

FACE FRAME LAYOUT
STANDING CUPBOARD

3

Cut the dadoes in the sides. The shelves and half-shelves are joined to the sides with ³/₄"-wide, ³/₈"-deep dadoes. Cut these with a dado cutter or a hand-held router. (If you use a router, clamp a straightedge to the stock to guide the tool.) Note that the dadoes that hold the half-shelves are *blind* — cut them 10" in from the back edges of the sides, then stop. Cut the other dadoes through to both the front and back edges. After you've made the dadoes, square the blind ends with a chisel.

4

Assemble the face frames. As shown, the face frames are assembled with wood plates or "biscuits." Use a plate joiner to cut the grooves for these plates. (See Figures 1 through 4.) If you don't have a plate joiner, you may also dowel the face frames together. Use a doweling guide to drill the dowel holes.

Lightly sand the inside edges of the frame parts. Apply glue to the adjoining ends, edges, and grooves (or dowel holes), insert the plates (or dowels), and clamp the parts together. Check that the frames are square as you tighten the clamps.

When the glue dries, sand the joints clean and flush.

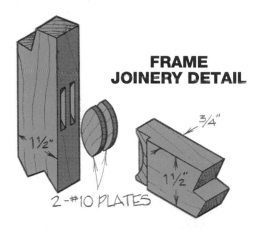

FRAME JOINERY DETAIL

1½"

3/4"

1½"

2 - #10 PLATES

1/Before cutting the plate grooves, lay out the parts on your workbench. Butt the adjoining ends and edges against one another, then mark across the joint with a pencil.

2/Using a square, transfer each pencil mark to the opposite face of the board.

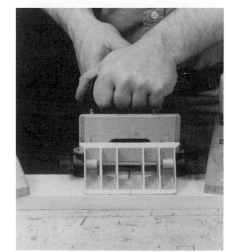

3/Cut grooves for the plates with a plate joiner. Adjust the joiner to cut the groove about ³/₁₆" below the face of the board. Line up the joiner with the mark, cut the groove, turn the board over, and repeat.

4/When you finish cutting, there should be two grooves in each adjoining end or edge. Insert the plates into these grooves.

5

Cut the notches and screw pockets in the spacers, if needed. The back ends of the drawer mount spacers for the countertop cupboard must be notched to fit around the top cleat, as shown in the *Countertop Cupboard/Section A.* Cut these notches with a band saw or a hand saw.

The countertop spacers also require screw pockets, so you can mount the countertop to the case. To make a screw pocket, tilt the table of a drill press at 15°, and attach a fence to the table to help support the stock. Place the stock on the drill press table, top edge down. Drill a 3/4″-diameter pocket in the side of the spacer, stopping about 1/2″ before the edge. Then drill a 3/16″ pilot hole through the center of the pocket. The pilot hole should exit the wood in the center of the top edge. (See Figure 5.)

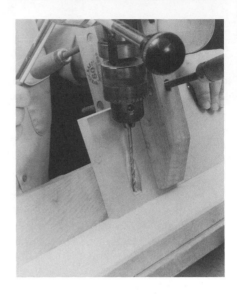

5/To make a screw pocket, drill angled holes into the side of a spacer.

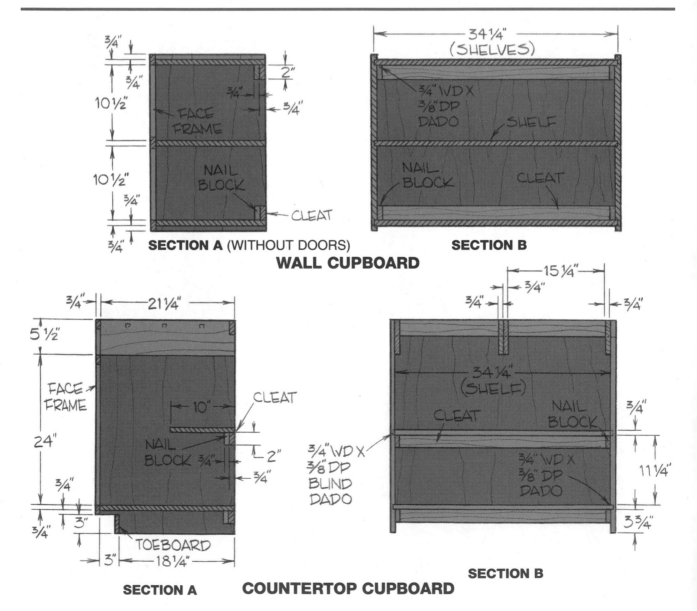

SECTION A (WITHOUT DOORS)   **SECTION B**

WALL CUPBOARD

SECTION A   **COUNTERTOP CUPBOARD**   **SECTION B**

6

Assemble the cases. Finish sand the face frames and toeboards, and lightly sand all the plywood surfaces inside and out. Mark the locations of the spacers and the nailing blocks on the sides of the cupboards. Attach the spacers and nailing blocks with glue and 4d finishing nails. Set the heads of the nails.

Note: 4d nails are 1½″ long. If you drive them straight into the wood and set the heads, the points will protrude from the opposite surface. To prevent this, drive the nails at an angle. Vary the angle back and forth to help hook the parts together.

Assemble the sides and shelves with #10 x 1½″ flathead wood screws and glue. Counterbore and countersink the heads of the screws. While the glue is still wet, attach the cleats, face frames, and toeboards with glue and nails. Make sure the cases are square before driving the nails into the face frames.

Set the heads of the nails, and cover them with wood putty. Cover the screw heads by gluing wooden plugs in the counterbores. When the glue and putty dry, sand all surfaces clean and flush.

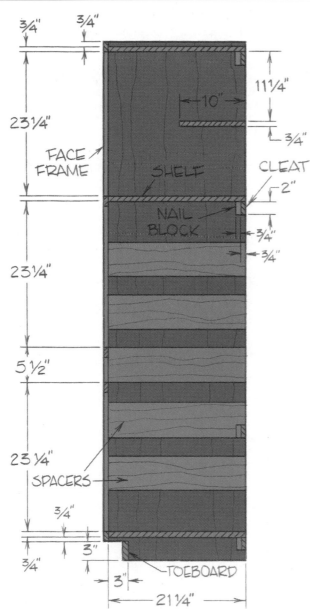

SECTION A
(WITHOUT DOORS AND DRAWER)

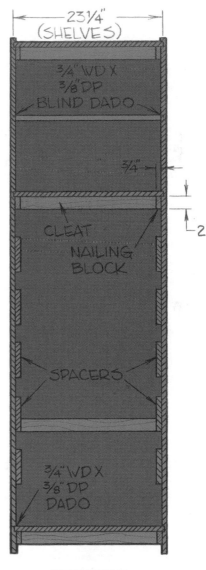

SECTION B

STANDING CUPBOARD

7 **Cover and install the countertop.** Glue the countertop parts face to face to make a single 1½″-thick plywood slab. Sand or saw the ends and edges flush. Cover the ends that will be visible on the installed countertop with oversize strips of plastic laminate. Use contact cement to attach the laminate, then trim the attached strip to size with a hand-held router and a trimmer bit. (See Figure 6.) Repeat for the edges, then the top surface.

Attach the countertop to the case by driving flathead screws up through the screw pockets in the spacers.

*6/When applying the plastic laminate, cover the ends first, then the edges, then the top surface. Trim each strip or sheet of laminate to size **after** you've glued it in place.*

8 **Install the cases.** Finish sand any plywood surfaces that will be visible on the installed cupboards. Find and mark the studs in the walls. (See Figures 7 and 8.) Then fasten the cases to the wall by driving lag screws through the cleats and into the studs, as shown in the *Installation Detail*. If you're fastening the cupboards to a masonry wall, install expandable lead anchors in the wall, then drive the lag screws through the cleats and into the anchors.

7/To find the studs in a frame wall without poking lots of holes in it, first make sure the power in the wall is shut off. Tap along the wall with a small hammer. Where the wall sounds solid, drill a ⅛″-diameter hole. If the drill meets resistance and brings up wood chips, then you've found a stud.

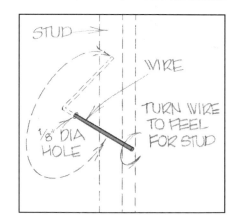

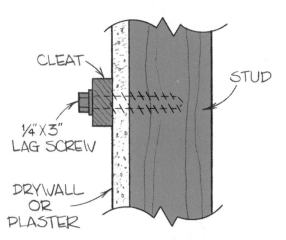

8/If the drill meets no resistance, you've missed the stud — but probably not by very much. Insert an L-shaped coat-hanger wire into the hole and feel around until you find the stud.

INSTALLATION DETAIL

9 **Cut the door, drawer, and bin parts.** Measure the openings in the cases and compare the dimensions to those of the doors, drawers, and bins. Chances are, these will have changed somewhat — this is normal with large case pieces. Make the necessary adjustments in the sizes of the doors, drawers, and bins, then cut the parts to size.

Note: As drawn, the drawers and bins are 1″ narrower than the openings. This allows for the thickness of two extension slides, one mounted on either side of each assembly. Most slides are ½″ thick; however, this thickness may vary depending on the brand. When determining the sizes of the drawer and bin parts, measure your slides as well as the openings.

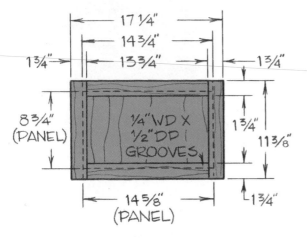

DOOR LAYOUT
WALL CUPBOARD

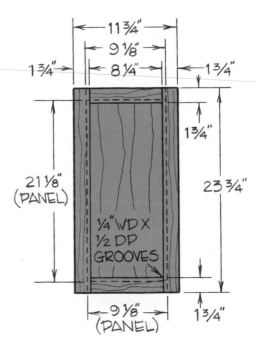

DOOR LAYOUT
STANDING CUPBOARD

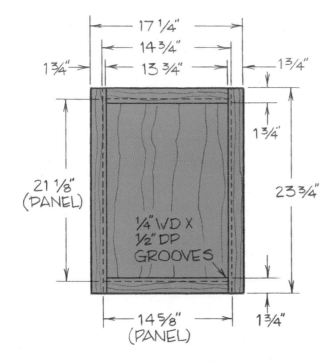

DOOR LAYOUT
COUNTERTOP CUPBOARD

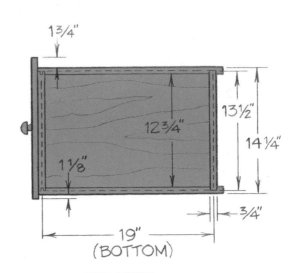

TOP VIEW

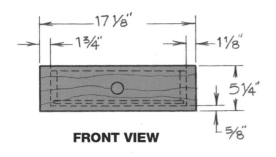

FRONT VIEW

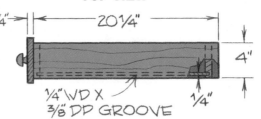

SIDE VIEW

COUNTERTOP CUPBOARD DRAWER

10 Make and install the drawers.

As shown in the *Drawer Joinery Detail* drawing, the front of each drawer is joined to the sides with ¼″-thick, ⅜″-long tongues and matching grooves. The back rests in ¾″-wide, ⅜″-deep dadoes in the sides. The bottom floats in ¼″-wide, ⅜″-deep grooves in the front, back, and sides. You can make all these joints with a dado cutter or a table-mounted router. (See Figures 9, 10, and 11.)

After cutting the joinery, finish sand the drawer parts. Glue the fronts, backs, and sides together, sliding the bottoms in place as you assemble the other parts. Do *not* glue the bottoms in the grooves; let them float. Glue the faces to the assembled drawers, centering them on the fronts; then install the drawer pulls.

Install the extension slides. Most slides separate so you can attach one part to the drawer and the other to

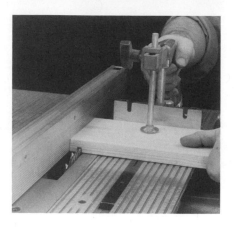

9/When cutting the tongue-and-groove joints that join the drawer fronts to the sides, position a fence ½″ away from a ¼″ cutter or bit. Cut a ¼″ dado in each drawer side, ½″ away from the front end. Use the fence **and** a miter gauge to guide the stock.

the case, then snap them back together again. Fit the drawer in the case, following the slide manufacturer's directions. Check the sliding action; if a drawer binds, adjust the slides.

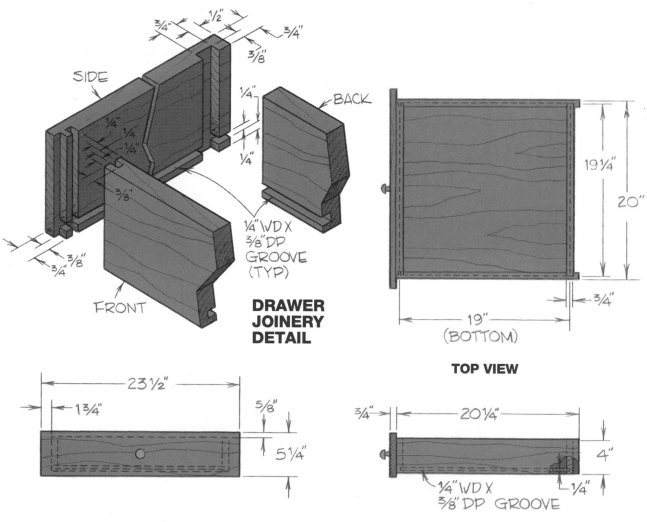

SIDE

BACK

¾″   ½″   ¾″

⅜″

¼″
¼″
¼″

¼″

¼″

⅜″

¼″ WD X ⅜″ DP GROOVE (TYP)

⅜″
¾″

FRONT

DRAWER JOINERY DETAIL

19¼″

20″

¾″

19″ (BOTTOM)

TOP VIEW

23½″

13¾″

5⅝″

5¼″

FRONT VIEW

¾″

20¼″

4″

¼″

¼″ WD X ⅜″ DP GROOVE

SIDE VIEW

STANDING CUPBOARD DRAWER

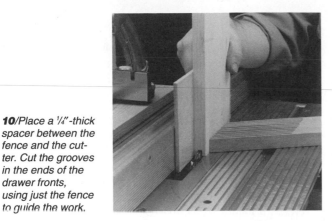

10/Place a ¼"-thick spacer between the fence and the cutter. Cut the grooves in the ends of the drawer fronts, using just the fence to guide the work.

11/Place a second ¼"-thick spacer between the first spacer and the cutter. Cut the rabbets in the ends of the drawer sides, using both the fence and the miter gauge to guide the stock. The rabbet and the dado will form a tongue.

11 **Make and install the bins.** The sides of the bins are joined with 45° miters, and the bottoms float in ¼"-wide, ⅜"-deep grooves. The rails are joined with corner laps, and the dowels that join the rails to the sides rest in ⅜"-diameter, ⅜"-deep holes.

Miter the adjoining ends of the sides, then cut the grooves in them with a dado cutter or a table-mounted router. Also cut ¾"-wide, ⅜"-deep rabbets in the ends of the rails to form the corner laps. Dry assemble the parts to check the fit.

Finish sand the parts of the bins. Assemble the sides with glue, sliding the bottoms into the grooves. Reinforce the miter joints with finishing nails, and set the heads. Also glue the rails together. When the glue dries, sand the joints clean and flush.

Drill dowel holes in the top edges of the sides and the bottom edges of the rails. Join the sides and rails, gluing ⅜"-diameter, 6"-long dowels in the holes.

Mount the bins in the standing cupboard on extension slides in the same manner that you installed the drawers.

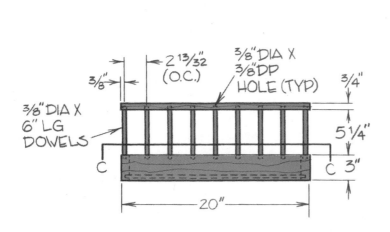

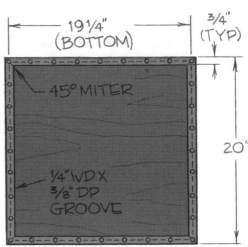

SIDE VIEW

SECTION C

BIN

12

Make and install the doors. The door rails, stiles, and panels are assembled with ¼"-thick, ½"-long tongues and matching grooves, as shown in the *Door Joinery Detail*. Using a dado cutter or a table-mounted router, cut grooves in the inside edges of both the rails and the stiles. Then cut tenons on the ends of the rails, fitting them to the grooves.

Finish sand the door parts. Assemble the rails and stiles with glue, sliding the panels into place. Make sure the doors are square when you clamp the parts together. After the glue dries, sand all the joints clean and flush.

Mount the doors on the face frame stiles with European-style surface-mounted cabinet hinges. Like the extension slides, these hinges come apart. Drill 1⅜"-diameter, ½"-deep holes in the door stile to mount one part of the hinge, and attach the other part to the face frame with screws, as shown in the *Door Mounting Detail*. To attach the doors to the cases, reassemble the hinges.

Note: These special hinges are available in some home improvement stores and from many woodworking mail-order suppliers. Here are two sources:

The Woodworkers' Store
21801 Industrial Blvd.
Rogers, MN 55374-9514

Woodworker's Supply
5604 Alameda Place
Albuquerque, NM 87113

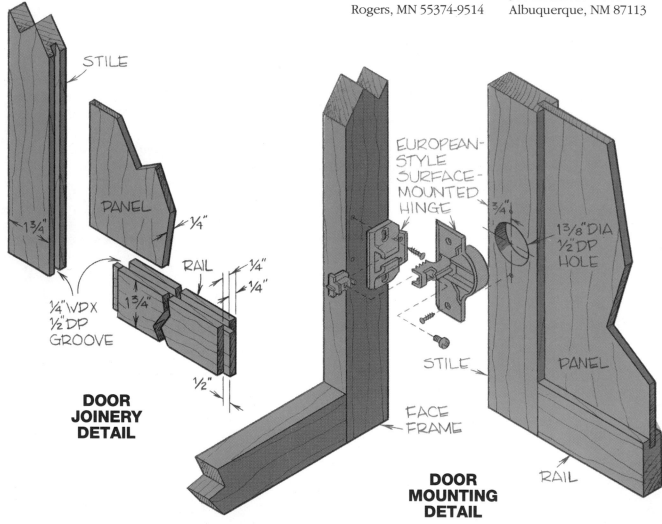

STILE

PANEL

¼"

1¾"

RAIL

¼"

¼"

¼"WDX
½"DP
GROOVE

1¾"

½"

**DOOR
JOINERY
DETAIL**

EUROPEAN-
STYLE
SURFACE-
MOUNTED
HINGE

¾"

1⅜"DIA
½"DP
HOLE

STILE

FACE
FRAME

PANEL

**DOOR
MOUNTING
DETAIL**

RAIL

13

Finish the cupboards. Remove the doors, drawers, and bins from the cases, and set the hardware aside. Do any necessary touch-up sanding to the wooden surfaces. Mask off the plastic laminate on the countertop so you don't get finish on it.

Then apply paint or finish to all outside (visible) surfaces. If you've installed these cupboards in a damp or humid location, you may also want to finish the insides of the cases and the backs of the doors. When the finish dries, replace the doors, drawers, and bins.

Wooden Icebox

During the late nineteenth and early twentieth centuries, most cooks kept their perishables in an icebox — an insulated wooden cupboard. Inside the cupboard, blocks of ice cooled the food and kept it from spoiling.

As more and more homes were wired for electricity, iceboxes were replaced by refrigerators. The old iceboxes, however, weren't necessarily discarded; folks found other uses for them. They gutted the boxes, removing the insulation and

drainage pans, then converted the wooden shells to linen presses, pantries, bookcases, toy chests, wardrobes, entertainment centers, and dozens of other storage units.

The small icebox shown was built in the early 1900s, and is used today

to hold stationery, envelopes, and other supplies in a home office. It's very simple to reproduce. Most of the parts are assembled with basic frame-and-panel joinery. These frames and panels form the front, back, sides, and doors of the box.

**DOORS
EXPLODED VIEW**

Materials List

FINISHED DIMENSIONS

A. Corner stiles (8) ³/₄″ x 2¹/₂″ x 41¹/₄″

B. Middle face
frame stile   ³/₄″ x 2¹/₂″ x 33³/₄″

C. Top face
frame rail   ³/₄″ x 2″ x 27¹/₂″

D. Middle face
frame rail   ³/₄″ x 2¹/₂″ x 13¹/₂″

E. Bottom face
frame rail   ³/₄″ x 3″ x 27¹/₂″

F. Short side/back
rails (14)   ³/₄″ x 2¹/₂″ x 12″

G. Bottom side
rails (2)   ³/₄″ x 6⁷/₈″ x 12″

H. Side panels* (10)   ¹/₄″ x 5¹/₈″ x 12″

J. Middle back
stile   ³/₄″ x 2¹/₂″ x 36¹/₄″

K. Top/bottom
back rails (2)   ³/₄″ x 2¹/₂″ x 25³/₄″

L. Top back
panels* (2)   ¹/₄″ x 12″ x 19″

M. Middle back
panels* (2)   ¹/₄″ x 12″ x 10³/₈″

N. Bottom back
panels* (2)   ¹/₄″ x 12″ x 3³/₈″

P. Divider stiles (2)   ³/₄″ x 2¹/₂″ x 34″

Q. Divider rails (3)   ³/₄″ x 2¹/₂″ x 11¹/₄″

R. Top divider
panel*   ¹/₄″ x 11¹/₄″ x 19″

S. Bottom divider
panel*   ¹/₄″ x 11¹/₄″ x 9″

T. Top   ³/₄″ x 17″ x 30¹/₂″

U. Cleats (4)   ³/₄″ x ³/₄″ x 15¹/₂″

V. Short shelf*   ³/₄″ x 15¹/₂″ x 14⁵/₈″

W. Long
shelves* (2)   ³/₄″ x 15¹/₂″ x 29¹/₂″

X. Adjustable shelves*
(optional)   ³/₄″ x 14″ x 15¹/₄″

Y. Large door
stiles (2)   ³/₄″ x 3″ x 32³/₄″

Z. Medium door
stiles (2)   ³/₄″ x 3″ x 20⁵/₈″

AA. Small door
stiles (2)   ³/₄″ x 3″ x 10⁵/₈″

BB. Door rails (7)   ³/₄″ x 3″ x 8¹/₂″

CC. Large door
panels* (2)   ¹/₄″ x 7¹/₄″ x 12⁵/₈″

DD. Medium door
panel*   ¹/₄″ x 7¹/₄″ x 15³/₈″

EE. Small door
panel*   ¹/₄″ x 7¹/₄″ x 5³/₈″

FF. Water door   ³/₄″ x 5″ x 25⁷/₈″

GG. Water door
mounts (2)   ³/₄″ x 2″ x 5¹/₄″

Make these parts from plywood.

HARDWARE

Offset icebox hinges and mounting
  screws (6)

Offset icebox latches and mounting
  screws (3)

Shelving support pins (for adjustable shelves — optional)

4d Finishing nails (¹/₄ lb.)

#10 x 1¹/₄″ Flathead wood screws
  (24–30)

¹/₄″ dia. x 1¹/₂″ Steel pins (2)

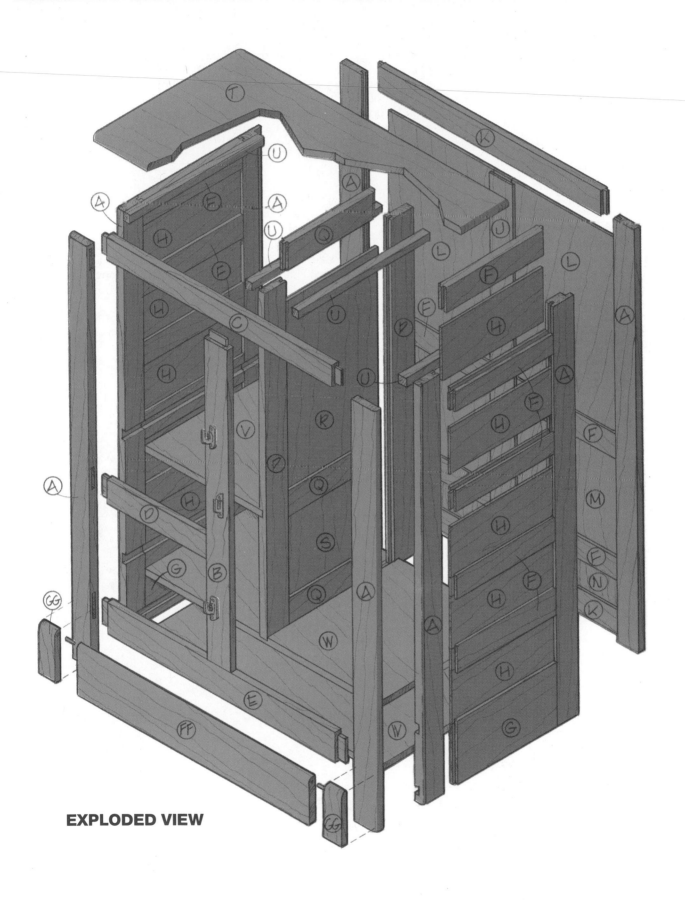

EXPLODED VIEW

1 Select the stock and cut the parts to size.

To make this project, you need about 34 board feet of 4/4 (four-quarters) stock, one 4' x 8' sheet of ³⁄₄" plywood, and two 4' x 8' sheets of ¹⁄₄" plywood. You can build the icebox from any kind of solid wood and cabinet-grade plywood, but iceboxes were traditionally made from oak. The icebox shown is made from white oak and oak-veneer plywood; many others were made from red oak.

When you have purchased the materials, plane all the 4/4 stock to ³⁄₄" thick. Cut all the parts to the sizes specified in the Materials List *except* the door parts. Don't cut these until after you've assembled the cabinet.

2 Cut the tongues and grooves in the side, back, and divider parts.

The sides, back, and inside divider are typical frame-and-panel assemblies — large, flat components made up of rails, stiles, and panels. These are assembled with tongue-and-groove joints.

Cut or rout ¹⁄₄"-wide, ³⁄₈"-deep grooves in the *inside* edges of all the rails and stiles that make up the back, sides, and divider, as shown in *Section A* and *Section B*. (See Figure 1.) Then cut ¹⁄₄"-thick, ³⁄₈"-long tongues on the ends of all the rails. (See Figure 2.) These tongues will fit into the grooves in the stiles.

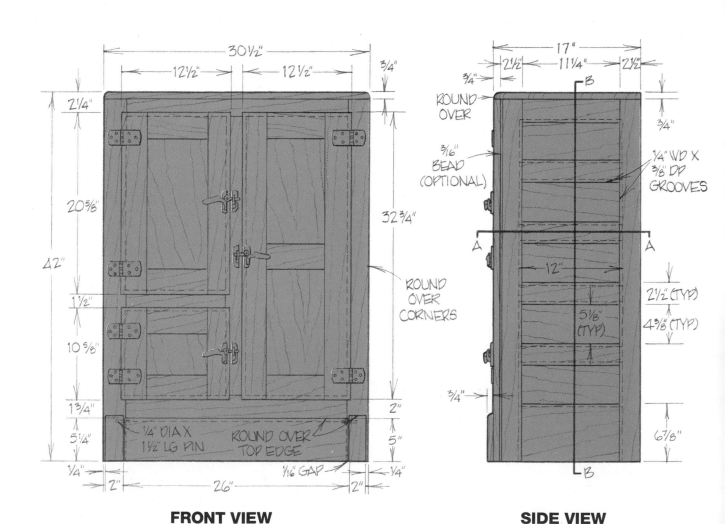

FRONT VIEW   **SIDE VIEW**

1/Using a dado cutter (shown) or a table-mounted router, cut ¼"-wide, ⅜"-deep grooves in the inside edges of the rails and stiles. These grooves should be centered in the edges.

2/Still using the same tool, cut a ⅜"-wide, ¼"-deep rabbet in both ends of each rail. Turn each board over and cut a second rabbet in the ends. Each pair of rabbets will form a ¼"-thick, ⅜"-long tongue. These tongues should fit snugly in the grooves.

3 Assemble the sides, back, and divider.

Dry assemble the rails, stiles, and panels, as shown in the *Side View, Back Layout,* and *Divider Layout.* The tongues and panels should fit snugly in the grooves, but not too tightly.

When you're satisfied that the joints fit properly, disassemble the parts. Finish sand the panels and the inside edges of the rails and stiles, but not the other surfaces. Reassemble the rails and stiles with glue, sliding the panels in place as you do so. Do *not* glue the panels in the grooves; let them float so they can expand and contract with changes in humidity.

Check that the side, back, and divider assemblies are square as you clamp them together. Using a wet rag, wipe away any excess glue that squeezes out of the joints. When the glue dries, sand the joints clean and flush.

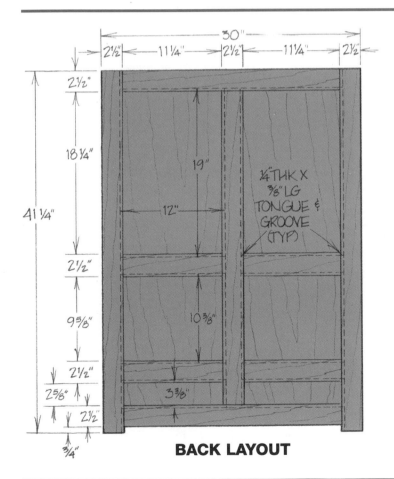

BACK LAYOUT

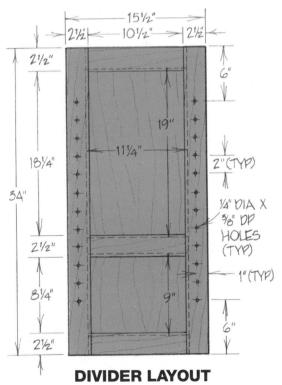

DIVIDER LAYOUT

4 Cut the rabbets and dadoes in the sides, back, divider, and shelves.

The sides, back, divider, and shelves all fit together with simple rabbets and dadoes. These must be cut *after* the frames and panels are assembled. (See Figure 3.) Here's a list:

- ³⁄₄″-wide, ¹⁄₂″-deep rabbets in the back stiles of the sides, as shown in *Section A*
- ³⁄₄″-wide, ¹⁄₄″-deep dadoes in the sides and divider to hold the shelves, as shown in *Section B*
- a ³⁄₄″-wide, ¹⁄₄″-deep dado in the upper long shelf to hold the divider, as shown in *Section B*

3/Using a dado cutter or a hand-held router, make the rabbets and dadoes in the sides, back, and divider. If you use a router (as shown), clamp a straight-edge to the stock to guide the tool.

5 Cut the mortises and tenons in the face frame parts.

The face frame parts are assembled with mortises and tenons, as shown in the *Face Frame Layout*. Make the ¹⁄₄″-wide, 1″-deep mortises first, then fit the tenons to them.

There are several ways to make the mortises. Here are two suggestions: (1) Drill a line of overlapping ¹⁄₄″-diameter holes to rough out each mortise, then clean up the sides and ends with a chisel. Or (2) rout the mortises on a table-mounted router, then square the ends with a chisel. (See Figures 4, 5, and 6.)

Make a ¹⁄₄″-thick, 1″-long tenon in a test piece with a dado cutter or a table-mounted router. (See Figure 7.) Fit it to one of the mortises. If the tenon is too tight, raise the cutter or router bit. If it's too loose, lower it.

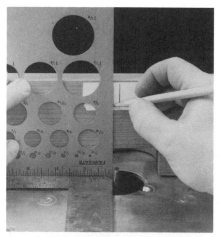

*4/To rout a mortise with a table-mounted router, you must know when to start and stop cutting. To help monitor the cut, mark the ends of the mortises on the **outside** edges of the boards, as well as the inside. Also, stick a piece of masking tape to the guide fence and mark the diameter of the router bit.*

5/Cut the mortise gradually, routing just ¹⁄₈″ – ¹⁄₄″ deeper with each pass. To start a pass, slowly lower the board onto the bit, keeping the face of the board pressed against the fence.

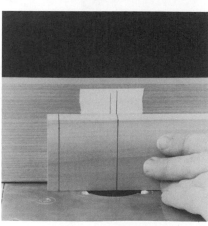

6/Feed the board left and right, keeping it pressed against the fence. As you feed the stock to the right, stop cutting when the left mark on the fence lines up with the left mark on the stock. When feeding it back to the left, stop cutting when the two right-hand marks line up.

7/To make the tenons in the ends of the face frame parts, cut 1″-wide, ¹⁄₄″-deep rabbets in all four surfaces of each part. These four rabbets will form a ¹⁄₄″-thick, 1″-long tenon.

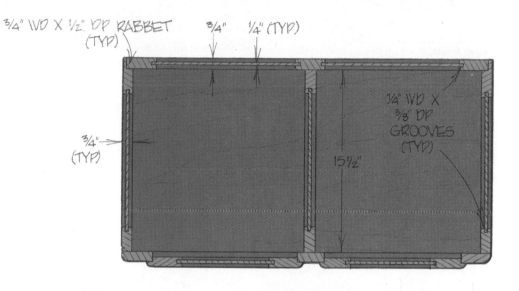

3/4" WD X 1/2" DP RABBET (TYP)

3/4"   1/4" (TYP)

1/4" WD X 3/8" DP GROOVES (TYP)

3/4" (TYP)

15 1/2"

SECTION A

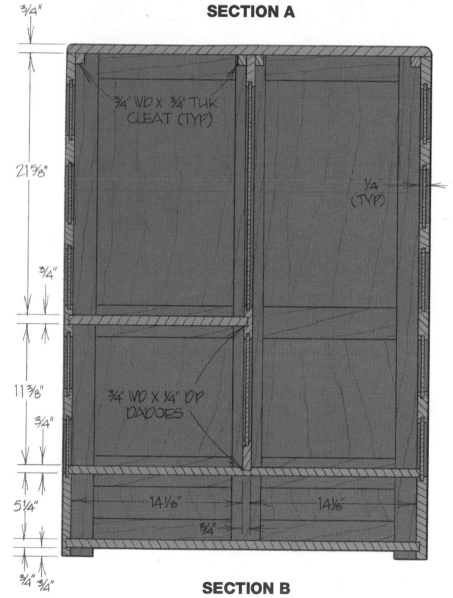

3/4"

3/4" WD X 3/4" THK CLEAT (TYP)

1/4" (TYP)

21 5/8"

3/4"

11 3/8"

3/4" WD X 1/4" DP DADOES

3/4"

5 1/4"

14 1/8"   14 1/8"

3/4"

3/4" 3/4"

SECTION B

6   ***Assemble the face frame.***   Finish sand just the inside edges of the face frame rails and stiles. Assemble the frame, gluing the tenons in the mor-tises. Check that the frame is square, and wipe away any excess glue. After the glue dries, sand the joints clean and flush.

7   ***Drill the holes for the shelving supports.***   If you want to install adjustable shelves inside the icebox, rest them on pin-style shelving supports. To hold the supports, drill rows of ¼"-diameter, ⅜"-deep holes along the inside faces of the divider stiles and side stiles, as shown in the *Divider Layout*. These holes should be spaced evenly, 2" apart.

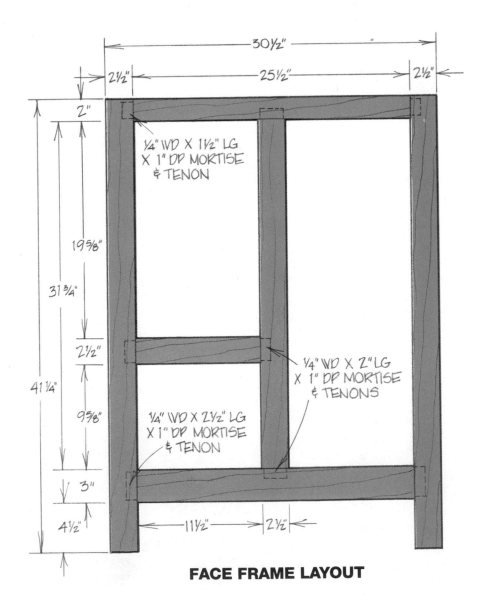

FACE FRAME LAYOUT

8

Assemble the case. Finish sand all the surfaces of the face frame, sides, back, divider, shelves, cleats, and top that you have not already sanded. Dry assemble the parts to check the fit of the joints. When you're satisfied they all fit properly, reassemble them with glue. Reinforce the glue joints with finishing nails, and set the heads.

> **TRY THIS!** Drive the nails at angles, and vary the angle back and forth with each nail. This will help hook the parts together.

Let the glue dry, then sand the joints clean and flush. Glue and screw the cleats to the inside surfaces of the sides and both sides of the divider, as shown in *Section B*. The top faces of the cleats should be flush with the top edges of the sides and divider.

Drill oversize pilot holes in the cleats, slightly larger than the screws you will use to attach the top. Put the top in place and secure it, driving the screws up through the cleats and into the top. Do *not* glue the top to the case. The screws in the oversize pilot holes will let it expand and contract; glue, on the other hand, would restrict the movement and cause the top to warp or split.

Sand the edges and ends of the top flush with the face frame, back, and sides.

9

Round the corners of the case. Using a hand-held router and a ½″ quarter-round bit, round over both ends and the front edge of the top.

Also round over the corners where the face frame joins the sides. Sand the rounded corners to remove any mill marks.

10

Make the doors. Measure the door openings in the case. If they have changed slightly from what is shown in the drawings, adjust the sizes of the doors accordingly. Then cut the parts for the doors.

Like the sides, back, and dividers, the doors are frame-and-panel assemblies. However, because the door frames must support their own weight (without being reinforced by adjoining parts), these are assembled with haunched mortises and tenons, as shown in the *Door Frame Assembly Detail.*

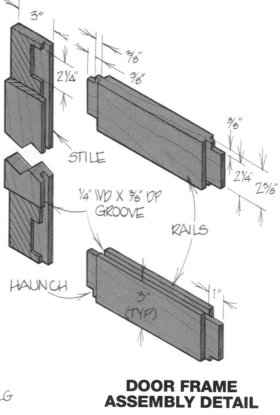

DOOR FRAME ASSEMBLY DETAIL

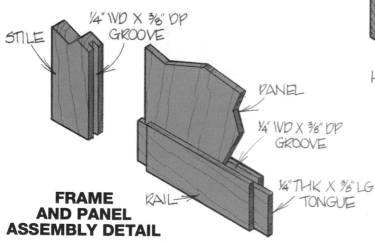

FRAME AND PANEL ASSEMBLY DETAIL

Making a haunched mortise-and-tenon joint combines the techniques you used in making the tongue-and-groove joints and the ordinary mortise-and-tenon joints.

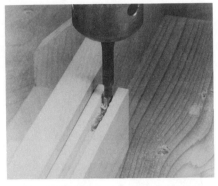

8/Rout or drill the mortises in the bottoms of the stile grooves. If you use a drill press, rough out each mortise by making a line of overlapping holes. Clean up the sides and the ends with a chisel.

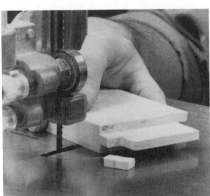

9/After making the tenons in the ends of the rails, cut a notch or "haunch" in the outside corner of each tenon.

First, cut or rout ¼"-wide, ⅜"-deep grooves in the inside edges of all the rails and stiles. Carefully measure and mark the positions of the ¼"-wide, 2¼"-long, 1"-deep mortises in the stile grooves. Cut them with a table-mounted router or drill press, and square the ends of the mortises with a chisel. Make ¼"-thick, 1"-long tenons in the ends of the rails, fitting them to the mortises. Finally, cut a ⅝"-long, ⅜"-deep notch or "haunch" in each tenon with a dovetail saw. (See Figures 8, 9, and 10.)

Finish sand the panels and the inside edges of the door stiles and rails. Assemble the door frames with glue, sliding the panels into place as you do so. As before, do *not* glue the panels in the grooves. Make sure the doors are square, let the glue dry, and sand the joints clean and flush.

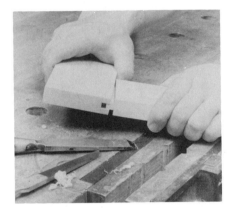
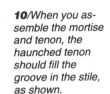

10/When you assemble the mortise and tenon, the haunched tenon should fill the groove in the stile, as shown.

11 **Cut the lips in the doors.** The icebox doors are lipped — rabbeted all the way around the perimeter. The shoulders of this rabbet sit inside the door opening, and the lips cover it.

Before making the lips, round over the outside ends and edges of each door with a router and a ⅜" quarter-round bit. Then cut ½"-wide, ⅜"-deep rabbets in the inside ends and edges of the doors, as shown in the *Door Edge Profile.*

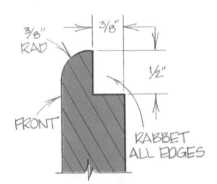

DOOR EDGE PROFILE

12 **Mount the doors on the icebox.** Finish sand the surfaces of the doors that still need it. Lay the icebox on its back, then lay the doors in place. Fasten the doors to the icebox with special icebox hinges and hold them closed with icebox latches. You can still buy this unusual hardware from many different sources.

Here are two:

The Woodworkers' Store
21801 Industrial Blvd.
Rogers, MN 55374-9514

The Renovator's Supply
Renovator's Old Mill
Miller's Falls, MA 01349

13

Make and mount the water door. The bottom compartment in the icebox once held a water tray, where water from the melting ice accumulated. This compartment is covered by a "water door" — a long board that pivots on two steel pins.

Round over the top edge of the water door, on both the inside and the outside surfaces, using a router and a ³/₈″ quarter-round bit. Also round over the top outside edges of the water door mounts.

Bore ¼″-diameter, ³/₄″-deep holes in the ends of the water door and the inside ends of the mounts, as shown in the *Front View*. Insert steel pins in these holes to make pivots.

Secure the water door mounts to the face frame stiles, driving screws through the stiles and into the mounts from the inside. Do *not* glue the mounts in place.

Test the action of the water door. It should pivot freely, without binding on the face frame. If it does bind, sand or file a little stock from the rounded top edge of the door.

14

Finish the icebox. Remove all the doors — including the water door — and set the hardware aside. Do any necessary touch-up sanding to wooden surfaces, then apply a finish. Coat all surfaces evenly, both inside and out. This will help keep the case and the doors from warping or distorting. When the finish dries, rub it out. Apply a coat of wax and buff. Finally, replace the doors.

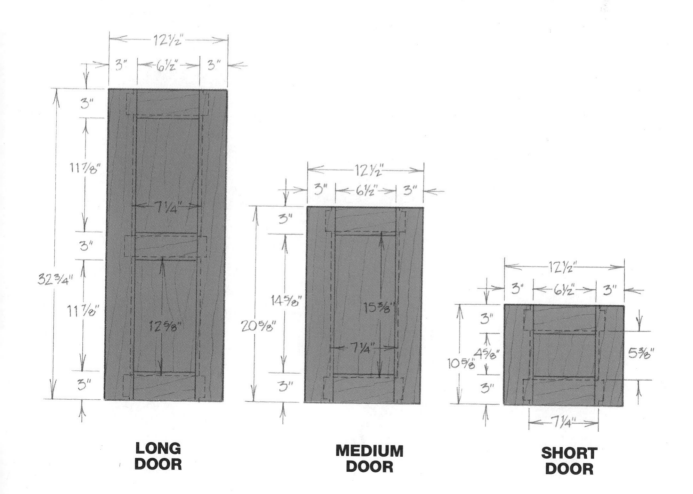

LONG DOOR

MEDIUM DOOR

SHORT DOOR

Slide-Top Box

A sliding dovetail is a fascinating way to attach a lid to a small box. If the box is made with precision, the sliding action of the dovetail has an enchanting feel — the lid slides on and off smoothly, and it becomes a joy just to open and close the box.

You can double this enchantment by adding a dovetailed drawer. The box shown is made from a single block of wood that was sliced into three pieces and dovetailed together. The box itself is just a solid board in which several recesses have been routed, and the top is a smaller piece that slides over the box. The drawer is a third slab that has been attached below the box. Slide the top sideways to access the box, or slide the box sideways to open the drawer.

Materials List

FINISHED DIMENSIONS

PARTS

A. Box   1″ x 3″ x 8″
B. Lid   ½″ x 3″ x 8″
C. Drawer   ¾″ x 3″ x 8″

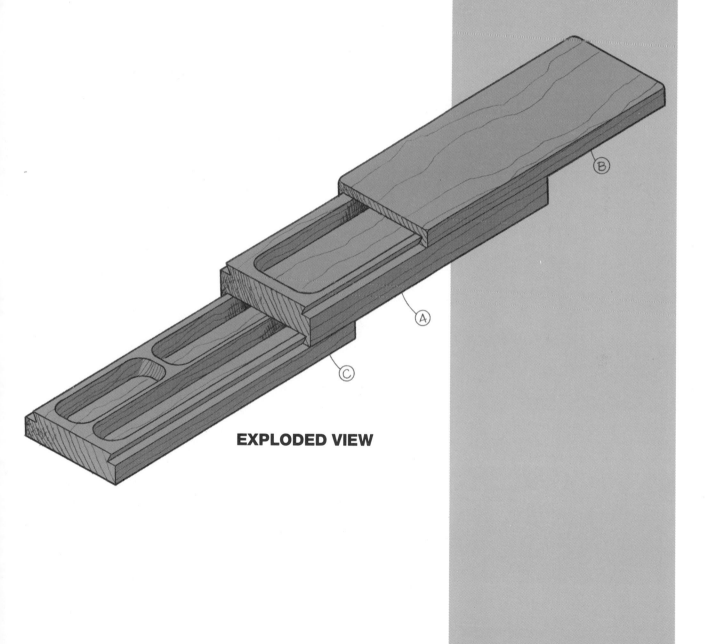

EXPLODED VIEW

Note: The measurements in the Materials List and on the drawings are just suggestions. You can make this project almost any size, and cut the box and drawer as deep or shallow as you wish. Furthermore, you can configure the recesses in the box and drawer any way you want.

1 Prepare the stock and cut the parts.

You can make a slide-top box from *any* kind or species of wood you want, as long as it's dry. Harder woods seem to work better — the sliding dovetails don't wear as quickly. If you intend to make this box from laminated wood, glue the stock together and let it dry for at least 24 hours. Plane and cut the wood into a rectangular block about 1″ longer and 1″ wider than you want to make the finished box. Slice the block into four pieces — lid, box, drawer, and test piece. (See Figure 1.)

1/Using a band saw, resaw the wood block into four parts — top, box, drawer, and test piece. The top should be thinner than the box and drawer. The thickness of the test piece won't matter.

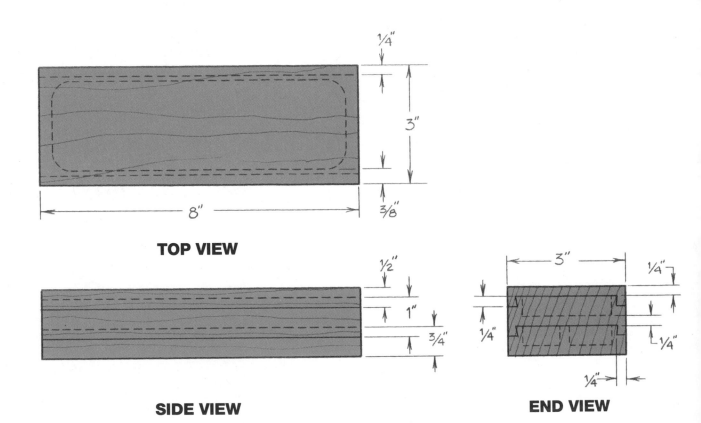

TOP VIEW

SIDE VIEW

END VIEW

2

Rout the recesses in the box and drawer. There are several ways to make the recesses in the box and drawer, but one of the easiest is to use a hand-held router in the same manner that you might rout a mortise for a hinge. Cut the recesses with a straight bit or core-box bit, guiding the router with a template. Attach a guide collar to the base of the router to ride along the sides of the template. (See Figure 2.)

Design the recesses you want to make in the box and drawer. Remember, the end walls should be no thinner than 1/4″, the side walls (where you'll cut the dovetails) no thinner than 3/8″, and the inside walls no thinner than 1/8″. The depth of the recesses is limited to the depth of cut of the router and router bit.

Make a template from 1/8″-thick tempered hardboard for each recess. The voids in these templates should be slightly larger than the recesses you want to cut. To calculate how much larger, subtract the diameter of the router bit from that of the guide collar. For instance, if

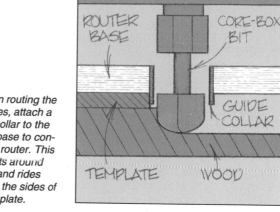

2/When routing the recesses, attach a guide collar to the router base to control the router. This collar fits around the bit and rides against the sides of the template.

you plan to use a 1/2″ core-box bit to cut the recesses and a 5/8″ collar to guide the router, cut the template 1/4″ wider and longer than the recess you will cut — (5/8″ - 1/2″) x 2 = 1/4″.

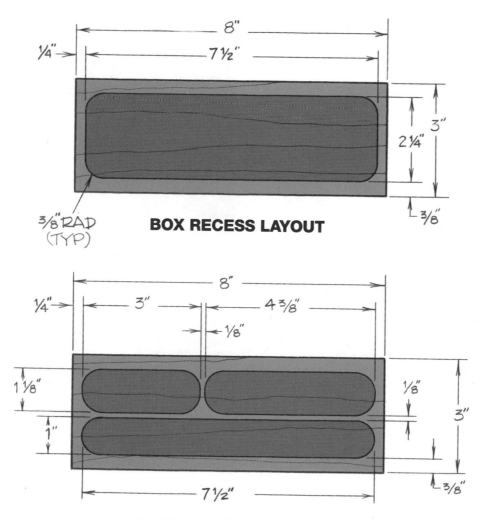

BOX RECESS LAYOUT

DRAWER RECESS LAYOUT

Lay out the templates on the blocks. Remember, these blocks are 1″ longer and wider than the completed box will be — the end walls should be 1¼″ wide and the side walls 1⅜″ wide on your layout. Also remember that you want the grain pattern and/or laminations to appear continuous on the completed box. Make sure that you cut the recesses in the proper faces of the box and drawer, so parts can be assembled in the correct configuration.

Stick the box or drawer to a template with double-faced carpet tape, centering the layout lines for the recess inside the void in the template. Clamp the block in a bench vise to hold it steady while you work. Rout the recess in several passes, cutting just ⅛″–¼″ deeper with each pass. (See Figure 3.) Remove the template and discard the tape. Repeat for each recess.

3/Rout each recess with a separate template. Because the interior walls of the box and drawer are fairly thin, you won't be able to make one template for all the recesses.

3   **Cut the blocks to size.** Stack the blocks, making sure the ends and the edges are flush. Also, arrange the blocks in the same configuration in which you want to assemble them, making sure the wood grains and/or laminations line up. Stick them together with double-faced carpet tape.

Cut the entire stack of blocks to the proper width and length at once, using a band saw. (See Figure 4.) Sand or plane the sawed edges smooth. Then take the stack apart and discard the tape.

4/After routing the recesses, stack the lid, box, drawer, and test piece together in the proper configura- tion. Cut them to the finished length and width, sawing all four parts at once.

4   **Cut the dovetail mortises.** A sliding dovetail joint consists of a mortise and a tenon. Like most mortise-and-tenon joints, it will be easier to make if you cut the mortises first, then fit the tenons to them.

The dovetail mortises are routed into the bottom surfaces of the lid and box using a table-mounted router.

To cut each mortise, mount a dovetail bit in the router and adjust it so it protrudes about ¼″ from the table. Starting in the *middle* of each part, cut a groove in the bottom face. Use a fence to guide the wood as you cut. Turn the part end for end (so the opposite side rests against the fence) and cut again. Move the fence about ¼″ *toward* the bit and repeat, making two more passes.

Continue until you've routed a broad dovetail groove in each part, leaving about ¼" of stock between the insides of the grooves and the outsides of the lid and box. (See Figure 5.)

5/To make the dovetail mortises, rout broad grooves in the bottom faces of the box and lid with a dovetail bit. Make these grooves in several passes, moving the fence slightly to cut the grooves wider.

5

Cut the dovetail tenons in the box and drawer. The dovetail tenons are cut in the tops of the box and drawer, using almost the very same setup you used to make the mortises. Without changing the height of the bit, adjust the position of the fence so the bit will shave about ¼" from the side of the blocks. To make a tenon, cut one side of each block, guiding it along the fence. Turn the piece end for end and make another cut. (See Figure 6.)

Cut a tenon in the test piece first, and fit it to one of the mortises. If it's too tight, move the fence *away* from the bit slightly, so you cut away more stock. If it's too loose, move the fence *toward* the bit. When the tenon on the test piece fits properly, cut the box and drawer.

6/To make a dovetail tenon, cut one side of a part, turn the wood end for end, and cut the other side. The two cuts will form the tenon.

6

Finish the box. Assemble the lid, box, and drawer. Finish sand the outside surfaces, making sure all the ends and edges are flush. (See Figure 7.) Disassemble the parts. Apply a *penetrating* finish, such as tung oil or Danish oil, to all surfaces. (Don't use a finish that builds up on the surface, such as varnish or polyurethane — these may interfere with the sliding action of the box.)

After the finish dries, rub it out and buff it with paste wax. Reassemble the parts.

7/Finish sand the the outside surfaces of the lid, box, and drawer with the parts assembled.

TRY THIS! If you wish, apply felt to the bottom of the recesses with contact cement. You might also cover the inside surfaces of the recesses with flocking. Flocking kits are available from some woodworking suppliers and at most hobby stores.

Quick Closet

Would you like additional closet space, without having to hassle with drywall or plaster work? Can you use a large storage cabinet that you can move about? Do you want a closet organizer that you don't have to build in place?

This versatile project provides all these things quickly and in expensively. It's just a large box with a hanger rod and several shelves — you can build it in a weekend from a few sheets of plywood. Yet it will afford as much storage as a full-size closet.

The closet shown is about the size of a large wardrobe. However, you can make it taller, shorter, wider, or narrower to fit a particular space simply by changing the length of several parts. You can add or subtract shelves and cubbyholes, mount it on casters, use different styles of doors, or leave it open. It can be easily adapted to your needs — and your budget. ✸

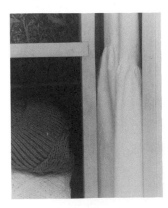

Materials List

FINISHED DIMENSIONS

PARTS

A.	Sides* (2)	$3/4''$ x $19^1/4''$ x $69''$
B.	Side trim (2)	$3/4''$ x $3/4''$ x $69''$
C.	Top*	$3/4''$ x $20^1/4''$ x $62''$
D.	Side top trim (2)	$3/4''$ x $3/4''$ x $21''$
E.	Front top trim	$3/4''$ x $3/4''$ x $63^1/2''$
F.	Top/middle shelves* (2)	$3/4''$ x $18^1/4''$ x $39^1/2''$
G.	Shelf trim (2)	$3/4''$ x $3/4''$ x $39^1/2''$
H.	Partition*	$3/4''$ x $12^3/4''$ x $18^1/4''$
J.	Partition trim	$3/4''$ x $3/4''$ x $12^3/4''$
K.	Divider*	$3/4''$ x $18^1/4''$ x $66^3/8''$
L.	Divider trim	$3/4''$ x $3/4''$ x $66^3/8''$
M.	Bottom shelf*	$3/4''$ x $19^1/2''$ x $60^3/4''$
N.	Long stop	$3/4''$ x $3/4''$ x $38^3/4''$
P.	Short stop	$3/4''$ x $3/4''$ x $20^1/2''$
Q.	Toeboard	$3/4''$ x $3''$ x $60''$
R.	Hanger blocks (4)	$3/4''$ x $3''$ x $3''$
S.	Long hanger rod	$1^1/4''$ dia. x $38^3/4''$
T.	Short hanger rod	$1^1/4''$ dia. x $20^1/2''$
U.	Left back**	$1/4''$ x $39^1/2''$ x $69^3/8''$
V.	Right back**	$1/4''$ x $21^1/4''$ x $69^3/8''$

*Make these parts from plywood.
**Make these parts from closet liner
particleboard, manufactured from
cedar shavings.

HARDWARE

#10 x $1^1/4''$ Flathead wood screws
  (42–48)
4d Finishing nails ($1/4$ lb.)
Bi-fold closet doors or shutters
  (optional)

EXPLODED VIEW

1 Determine the size and configuration of the closet.

Before you purchase materials, decide how to adapt the closet to your own needs and tastes.

First, decide how to configure the closet. This depends on what you want to put in it. As designed, the closet will hold a variety of clothes. There is an angled shelf for shoes, cubbyholes for sweaters, a shelf for accessories, a short hanging space for shirts, pants, and skirts, and a longer hanging space for dresses and coats. However, if you need to store just one or two types of clothes, you may want to add, subtract, or rearrange shelves, cubbyholes, and hanger rods.

Next, determine whether the closet will be open or closed. If you use this as an insert in an existing closet, you can leave it open. But if it stands alone in a room,

you'll probably want to add a door or curtain. You can use a ready-made folding closet door (as shown), make a folding door from shutters, make your own door, or hang a simple cloth curtain.

Finally, decide what size to make the closet. This depends on how much stuff you want to put in the closet, where you want to put it, and what sort of doors you're using. Folding doors and shutters come in standard sizes, and the size of the closet will have to be adjusted to fit these.

When you've determined how you'll build the closet, draw a sketch or plan. This doesn't need to be as detailed as the drawings you see here, but it should provide an adequate guide for determining the amount of materials, cutting them to size, and making the joinery.

2 Select the stock and cut the parts to size.

To make this project as shown, you need three 4' x 8' sheets of ³/₄" plywood, two 4' x 8' sheets of ¹/₄" cedar closet liner, 8 board feet of 4/4 (four-quarters) lumber, and one 1¹/₄"-diameter, 8'-long closet pole. You can use any kind of cabinet-grade wood and plywood that you prefer, but the wood species should match the

plywood veneer. The closet shown is made from birch and birch-veneer plywood.

After purchasing the stock, plane the 4/4 wood to a little over ³/₄" thick — about ²⁵/₃₂". Rip the trim parts you need, and cut them about 1" longer than specified in the Materials List. Plane the remaining stock to ³/₄" thick, and cut the hanger blocks, stops, and toeboard. Also cut the plywood and particleboard parts to size.

3 Trim the plywood.

Miter the adjoining ends of the top trim and glue them to the front edge and ends of the top. Also glue the trim to the front edges

of the sides, divider, shelves, and partition. Wipe any excess glue with a wet rag before it dries.

TRY THIS! You can hold the trim in place with strips of masking tape, spaced every 2"–3", while the glue dries. Masking tape is slightly elastic, and each strip will apply a little pressure to the joint. If you use enough strips, you can apply the pressure needed to get a good glue bond.

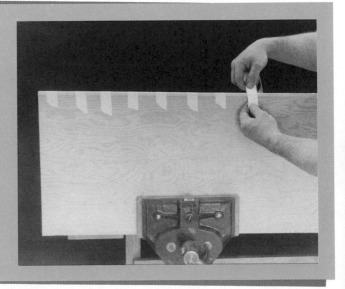

After the glue dries, use a cabinet scraper to shave the trim until the faces are flush with the faces of the plywood. (See Figure 1.) Where the trim is long, cut it flush with the edge of the plywood, using a dovetail saw.

1/The trim should be slightly thicker than the plywood. After fastening it in place, plane the trim with a cabinet scraper until the two parts are flush. Be careful not to scrape through the plywood veneer.

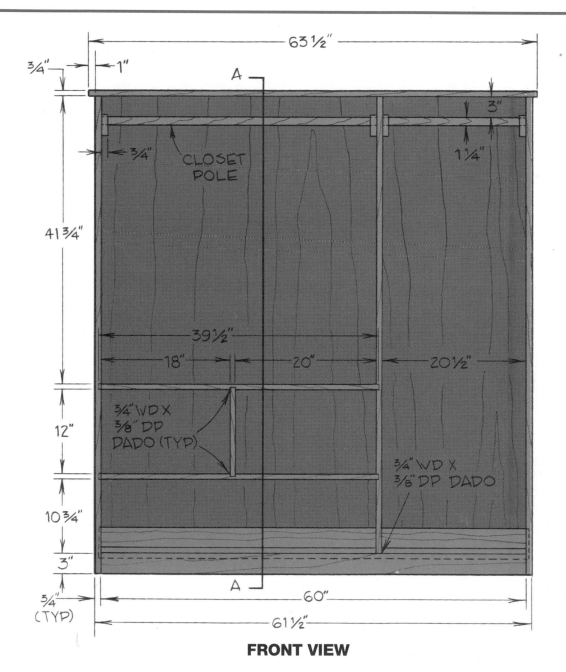

CLOSET POLE

¾" WD X ⅜" DP DADO (TYP)

¾" WD X ⅜" DP DADO

63½"
¾"   1"
3"
¾"
1¼"
41¾"
39½"
18"   20"   20½"
12"
10¾"
3"
¾" (TYP)
A
A
60"
61½"

FRONT VIEW

4 Cut the joinery in the top, sides, and divider.

The parts of the closet are assembled with rabbets and dadoes. Make these joints with a dado cutter or a router:

- ¼"-wide, ⅜"-deep rabbets in the back edges of the sides to hold the back parts, as shown in the *Left Side Layout*
- ¾"-wide, ⅜"-deep dadoes in the left side and the divider, to hold the top and middle shelves, as shown in the *Left Side Layout* and *Divider Layout*
- a ¾"-wide, ⅜"-deep dado in the bottom shelf to hold the divider, as shown in the *Front View*
- ¾"-wide, ⅜"-deep dadoes in the sides, angled 10° off perpendicular, to hold the bottom shelf, as shown in the *Left Side Layout*

Perhaps the best tools for making the angled dadoes are a hand-held router and a ¾" straight bit. Clamp a

2/Cut the angled dadoes with a hand-held router, using a straightedge to guide the tool. Make each dado in several passes, cutting just ⅛"–¼" deeper with each pass.

straightedge to the stock to guide the router, then cut the dadoes, holding the router firmly against the straightedge. (See Figure 2.)

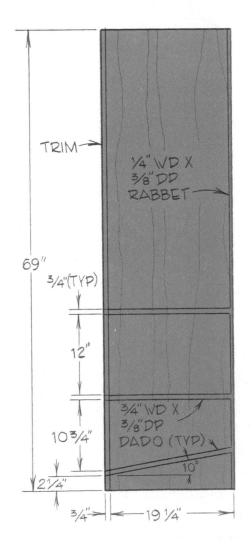

TRIM →

¼" WD X ⅜" DD RABBET →

69"

¾" (TYP)

12"

¾" WD X ⅜" DP DADO (TYP)

10¾"

10°

2¼"

¾" — 19¼"

LEFT SIDE LAYOUT

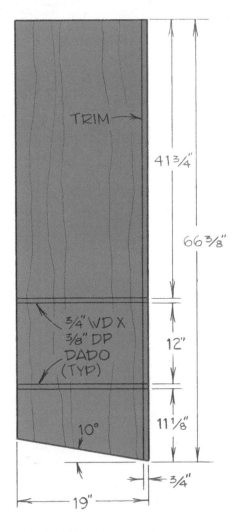

TRIM →

41¾"

66⅜"

¾" WD X ⅜" DP DADO (TYP)

12"

10°

11⅛"

¾"

19"

DIVIDER LAYOUT

5. Make the hanger blocks.

The hanger rods are suspended by hanger blocks — small blocks of wood with notches in the top edges. To make the notches, drill a 1¼″-diameter hole in each block. Open up this hole to the top edge with a band saw or saber saw. (See Figure 3.)

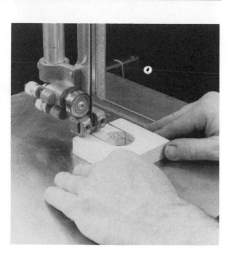

3/To make the notch in a hanger block, first drill a hole in the block. Remove the waste between the hole and the top edge with a band saw or saber saw.

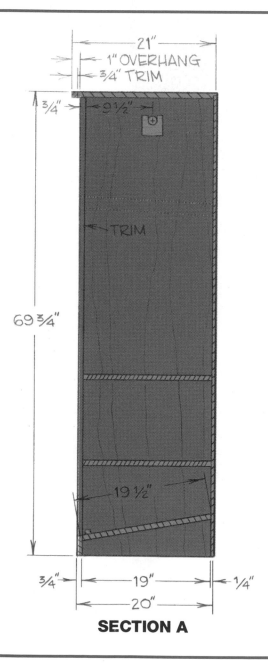

21″
1″ OVERHANG
¾″ TRIM
¾″
9½″
TRIM
69¾″
19½″
¾″   19″   ¼″
20″

SECTION A

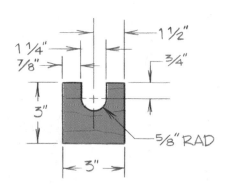

1¼″
7⁄8″
1½″
¾″
3″
3″
5⁄8″ RAD

HANGER BLOCK DETAIL

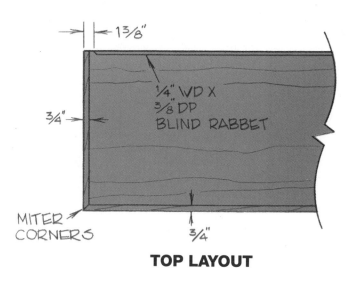

1³⁄8″
¼″ WD X
³⁄8″ DP
BLIND RABBET
¾″
MITER CORNERS
¾″

TOP LAYOUT

6

Assemble the closet. With a helper, dry assemble the parts of the closet to check the fit of the joints. When you're satisfied that they all fit, disassemble the parts and finish sand all surfaces *except* the back parts. Don't bother to finish sand these — the particleboard is too rough.

Glue the sides, top, and bottom shelf together to make a big box. Reinforce the glue joints with wood screws. Counterbore and countersink the heads of the screws — later, you'll cover the heads with wooden plugs to hide them.

Rest the assembly on its back edges and add parts in the following order, fastening them together with glue and screws:

- Attach the divider to the top and bottom shelves.
- Attach the top and middle shelves to the left side and the divider.
- Attach the partition to the shelves.
- Attach the toeboard to the bottom shelf and the sides.

Once again, counterbore and countersink all screws.

Turn the assembly over on its front edges and attach the back panels with glue and finishing nails. Set the heads of the nails.

Set the closet upright. Using glue and nails, attach the stops to the bottom shelf and the hanger blocks to the sides and divider. Make sure the notches in the hanger blocks face up. Once again, set the heads of the nails.

Glue wooden plugs in the counterbores to hide all the visible screwheads. Also, cover the heads of the nails with putty. Let the glue and putty dry, then sand the plugs and the hardened putty flush with the wood surface.

Rest the hanger rods in the notches in the hanger blocks. Do *not* glue them in place. You may want to remove the hanger rods and replace them with shelves sometime in the future.

7

Install doors on the closet. If you wish to install doors or shutters on the closet, do so at this time. The procedure will differ depending on the type and the brand of door you choose — follow the manufacturer's instructions. (See Figure 4.)

Note: You should purchase these doors and study the installation procedures *before* you build the closet. That way, you can design and build the closet to fit the doors.

4/If you wish, install folding or sliding doors in the closet opening.

8

Paint or finish the closet. Remove the doors and hanger rods, and set the hardware aside (if there is any). Do any necessary touch-up sanding, then paint the closet or apply a finish. Do *not* paint the back panels — this would seal the aromatic cedar. Let the paint or finish dry, then replace the hanger rods and doors.

Wardrobe

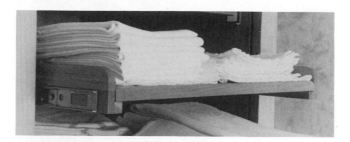

*B*uilt-in closets are a fairly recent innovation; before the late nineteenth century, most folks hung their clothes in large standing cupboards. The French called this piece an *armoire.* To the Germans, it was a *Schrank,* and to the Dutch, a *kas.* The Spanish called it a *trastero,* and the English, a *clothespress* or *wardrobe.*

Traditionally, furnituremakers built wardrobes with one or two drawers beneath the clothes cupboard. They also fitted the cupboard with several shelves if the client requested them. These additions increased the versatility of the piece.

The wardrobe shown was designed and built by Marian Curry of Cincinnati, Ohio, for her daughter. Marian followed the traditional formula, but she added some contemporary twists to make this old piece more useful in a modern home. Since her daughter has plenty of closet space, Marian fitted the cupboard with eight slide-out shelves, so it can be used to organize sweaters, bedding, towels, linens, and shoes. ●

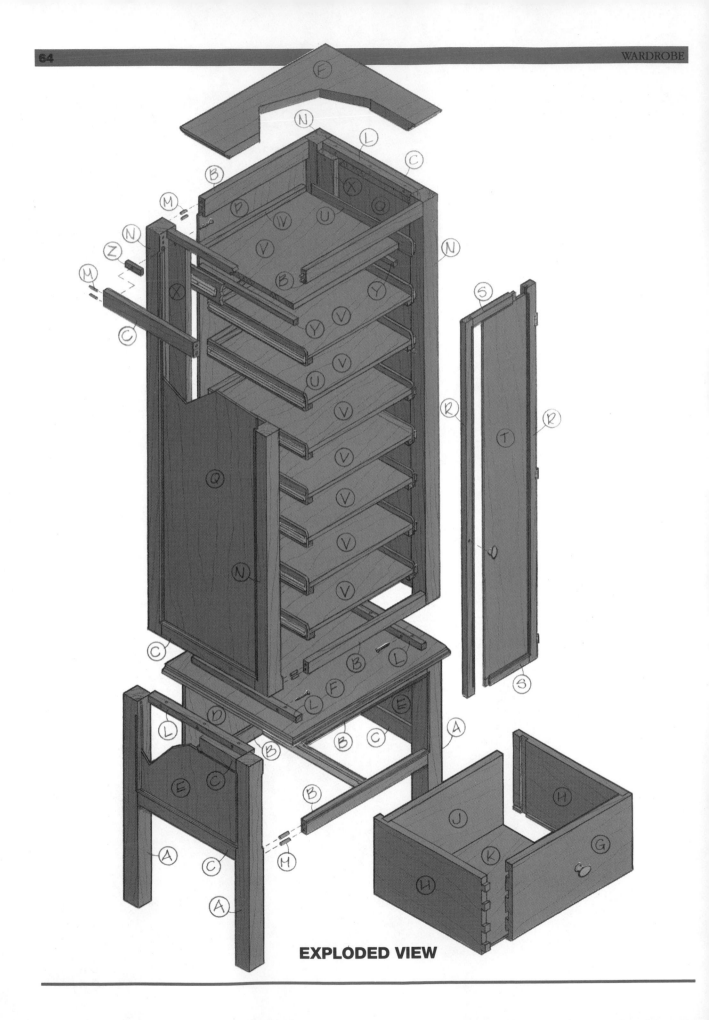

EXPLODED VIEW

Materials List

FINISHED DIMENSIONS

PARTS

Stand

A. Legs (4) $1^7/8'' \times 1^7/8'' \times 24''$

B. Front/back rails (4) $3/4'' \times 1^1/2'' \times 19^1/8''$

C. Side rails (4) $3/4'' \times 1^1/2'' \times 12^1/8''$

D. Back stand panel* $1/4'' \times 9^{11}/16'' \times 19^3/4''$

E. Side stand panels* (2) $1/4'' \times 9^{11}/16'' \times 12^3/4''$

F. Top $3/4'' \times 16^3/8'' \times 23^7/8''$

G. Drawer front $3/4'' \times 9'' \times 19^1/8''$

H. Drawer sides (2) $3/4'' \times 9'' \times 15''$

J. Drawer back $3/4'' \times 8^1/2'' \times 18^3/8''$

K. Drawer bottom* $1/4'' \times 14^1/4'' \times 18^3/8''$

L. Cleats (2) $3/4'' \times 3/4'' \times 12^1/8''$

M. Dowels (32) $3/8''$ dia. x $2''$

Case

B. Front/back rails (4) $3/4'' \times 1^1/2'' \times 19^1/8''$

C. Side rails (4) $3/4'' \times 1^1/2'' \times 12^1/8''$

F. Top $3/4'' \times 16^3/8'' \times 23^7/8''$

L. Cleats (4) $3/4'' \times 3/4'' \times 12^1/8''$

M. Dowels (32) $3/8''$ dia. x $2''$

N. Stiles (4) $1^7/8'' \times 1^7/8'' \times 47''$

P. Back case panel* $1/4'' \times 19^3/4'' \times 44^{11}/16''$

Q. Side stand panels* (2) $1/4'' \times 12^3/4'' \times 44^{11}/16''$

R. Door stiles (4) $3/4'' \times 1^1/2'' \times 44''$

S. Door rails (4) $3/4'' \times 1^1/2'' \times 7^5/16''$

T. Door panels* (2) $1/4'' \times 7^1/4'' \times 41^{11}/16''$

U. Shelf sides (16) $3/8'' \times 2^1/4'' \times 14^3/8''$

V. Shelf bottoms (8) $3/4'' \times 14^3/8'' \times 17^3/8''$

W. Shelf backs (8) $3/4'' \times 3/4'' \times 17^3/8''$

X. Shelf slide mounts (2) $3/4'' \times 1^1/2'' \times 45^1/2''$

Y. Shelf cleats (16) $3/4'' \times 3/4'' \times 14^3/8''$

Z. Spacers (4) $3/8'' \times 3/4'' \times 1^1/2''$

Make these parts from plywood.

HARDWARE

Stand

#10 x $1^1/4''$ Flathead wood screws (12)

14" Bottom-mounted drawer slide and mounting screws

Drawer pull

Case

#10 x $1^1/4''$ Flathead wood screws (24)

#10 x $1^1/2''$ Flathead wood screws (4)

14" Side-mounted extension slides and mounting screws (16)

Door pulls (2)

Bullet catches and latches (4)

---

1 **Select the stock and cut the parts to size.** To make this project, you need about 42 board feet of 4/4 (four-quarters) stock, 10 board feet of 8/4 (eight-quarters) stock, and one 4' x 8' sheet of $1/4''$ plywood. You can make this project from almost any cabinet-grade hardwood and plywood, but the plywood veneer should match the wood species. The wardrobe shown is made from mahogany and mahogany-veneer plywood.

When you have selected the materials, resaw 4 board feet of 4/4 stock in half and plane it to $3/8''$ thick. Cut the spacers to size, and set aside the rest of the $3/8''$ stock for the shelf sides. Plane the remaining 4/4 stock to $3/4''$ thick, and glue up the boards needed to make the wide parts — the tops and shelf bottoms. Cut the $3/4''$-thick wooden parts and $1/4''$ plywood parts to size, *except* the drawer, door, and shelf parts. Wait until you have made the case to cut these parts.

From 8/4 stock, cut four rough legs about 25" long, and four stiles about 48" long. Joint two adjacent faces on each part to make them precisely 90° from one another, then plane the remaining two faces so the blank is $1^7/8''$ square. Cut the legs and stiles to length.

2 **Drill the dowel holes in the legs, rails, and stiles.** The legs, rails, and stiles of the wardrobe are joined with $3/8''$-diameter, 2"-long dowels — two per joint. To seat these dowels, you must drill $3/8''$-diameter, 1"-deep holes in the ends of the rails and in the adjoining faces of the legs and stiles.

Measure and mark the locations of the dowels on the rails, stiles, and legs. Remember, when the rails are joined to the other parts, the outside faces must be flush. Drill the holes in the legs and stiles on a drill press, using a fence to help position the workpieces.

Drill the ends of the rails on a horizontal boring machine if you have one. Otherwise, make them with a portable power drill. (See Figures 1 and 2.) It won't matter if the dowel holes in the rails are a few degrees off parallel, as long as they're positioned accurately.

1/If you have a machine that will bore horizontal holes, use it to make the dowel holes in the ends of the rails. Most multi-purpose tools have this capacity. You can also purchase horizontal boring accessories for some radial arm saws and lathes.

2/If you don't have a horizontal boring tool, clamp the rails to the workbench and bore the ends with a portable power drill. Use a stop collar to stop the holes at the proper depth. As you work, keep the bit reasonably parallel to the length of the rails, but don't worry if you're a few degrees off.

3 **Drill the holes in the cleats.** The shelves, stand, and case are all assembled with cleats and screws. While you're set up for drilling, drill and countersink 3/16″-diameter pilot holes in the cleats. The holes are slightly larger than the shanks of the screws — this arrangement will allow the tops and shelves to expand and contract with changes in temperature and humidity.

Drill three holes along the lengths of 16 of these cleats. In each of the remaining 6, drill three holes along one face, turn the cleat 90°, and drill another three. The two sets of holes should cross at right angles in the cleat, but they must not intersect. You'll use the three-hole cleats to make the shelves, and the six-hole cleats to attach the stand and case to the tops.

4 **Cut the grooves in the rails, legs, and stiles.** The back and side panels rest in 1/4″-wide, 3/8″-deep grooves. The grooves in the rails are open, but those in the legs and stiles are double-blind — closed at *both* ends. You can make the open grooves with either a dado cutter or table-mounted router. However, you'll find a router is the best tool for making blind joints.

When making either type of groove, use a fence to guide the work. Before you cut the blind grooves, stick a piece of masking tape to the work surface in front of the bit. Using a square, mark the left and right sides (the diameter) of the bit on the tape, 1⅞″ away from the fence. Also mark the beginnings and ends of the grooves on *all four faces* of the board, including those faces that you don't intend to cut. (See Figure 3.)

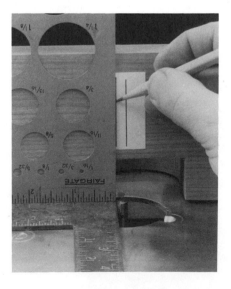

3/To rout a blind groove on a router table, you must know where to start and stop cutting. Since neither the bit nor the cut will be visible as you work, mark the diameter of the bit on the worktable. Mark the blind ends of the grooves on all four faces of the boards.

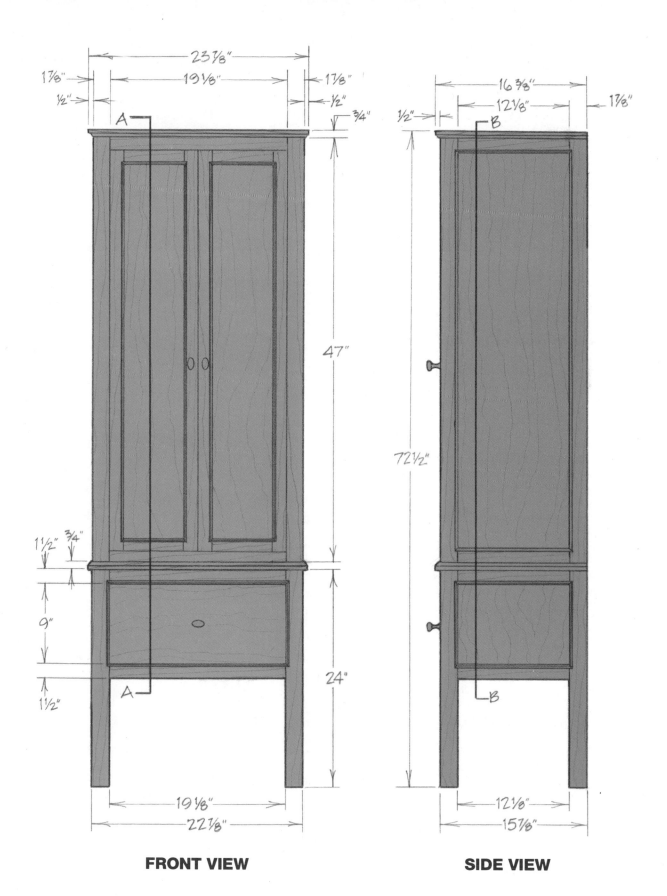

FRONT VIEW

SIDE VIEW

To make each groove, slowly lower the leg or stile onto the bit, keeping one surface pressed against the fence. Move the board to the right until the left-hand mark on the table lines up with the layout line that indicates the left end of the groove. (See Figure 4.) Move the board back toward the right and line up the two right-hand marks. While you work, keep the board firmly against the fence.

4/When you make a blind groove, stop cutting when the layout line that indicates the end of the groove is lined up with the appropriate mark on the worktable.

5 Shape the top, rails, stiles, and legs.

The front and side ends of the top are shaped as shown in the *Top Edge Profile*. The inside edges of the rails, stiles, and legs are cut with decorative beads, as shown in the *Front View* and *Side View*. Shape the top with a router or shaper and a ½″ quarter-round bit. Cut the beads in the other parts with a router and a piloted ¼″ quarter-round bit.

To cut the small beads, you must first dry assemble the parts to make a frame. Clamp the frame to your workbench, cut the inside edges, and square the corners with a carving chisel. (See Figure 5.) Then dismantle the frame so you can use the parts in other frames: For example, assemble the right legs and right side stiles to make the right stand frame. After cutting and squaring the beads, take the frame apart and assemble the front stand frame. Repeat this procedure for the left stand frame, back stand frame, right case frame, back case frame, and left case frame. Do *not* shape the inside edges of the front case frame — this is where you will mount the doors.

TRY THIS! You can also use a scratch stock to cut these small beads. Refer to Making and Using a Scratch Stock beginning on page 74.

5/When you rout the small beads, the router bit will leave a rounded shape in the corners. Using a small chisel, carve these so the beads appear to meet in a miter joint.

6 Assemble the stand and case.

Finish sand the legs, rails, stiles, tops, and panels. Lightly sand the six-hole cleats, spacers, and shelf slide mounts. Assemble the legs, stiles, and side rails with dowels and glue, making four side assemblies. Slide the side panels in place as you assemble these parts, but do *not* glue them in their grooves; let them float. As you clamp the parts together, make sure each of the assemblies is square.

When the glue dries, secure the cleats to both the case and the stand side assemblies with #10 x 1¼″ flathead wood screws. Then attach the spacers and shelf slide mounts to the case side assemblies with #10 x 1½″ flathead wood screws. Countersink the heads of the screws.

Attach the side assemblies, front rails, and back rails to one another with dowels and glue. As you do so, slide the back panels in place. Once again, do *not* glue the panels in their grooves. Make sure the case and stand assemblies are square as you clamp them together.

Turn the stand top upside down on the workbench, and place the stand assembly upside down upon it. Secure the stand to the top by driving screws through the cleats. Fasten the case to the case top in the same way. Then attach the case to the stand top with screws.

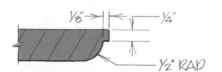

TOP EDGE PROFILE

1/8"   1/4"

1/2" RAD

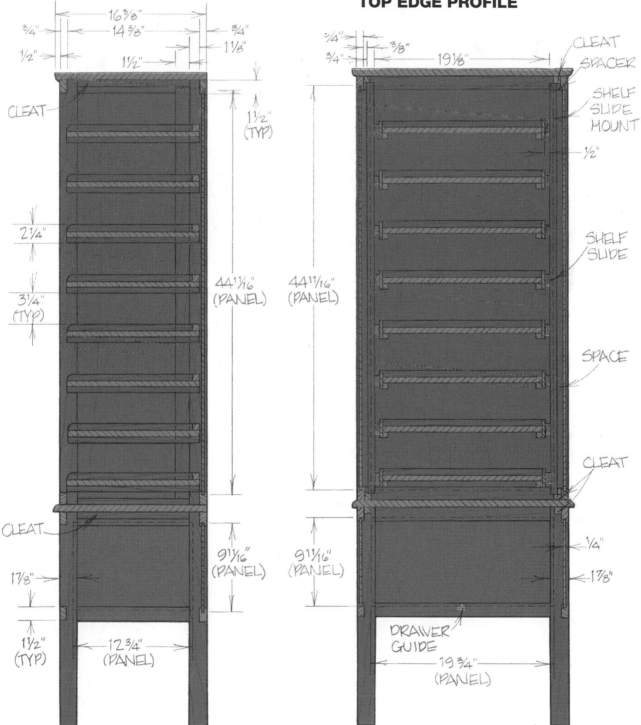

16 3/8"
14 3/8"
3/4"   3/4"
1/2"   1 1/8"
1 1/2"

CLEAT

1 1/2"
(TYP)

2 1/4"

3 1/4"
(TYP)

44 11/16"
(PANEL)

CLEAT

9 11/16"
(PANEL)

1 7/8"

1 1/2"
(TYP)   12 3/4"
(PANEL)

SECTION A
(WITHOUT
DOORS AND DRAWERS)

1/4"
3/4"   3/8"   19 1/8"

CLEAT
SPACER

SHELF
SLIDE
MOUNT

1/2"

SHELF
SLIDE

SPACE

CLEAT

44 11/16"
(PANEL)

9 11/16"
(PANEL)

1/4"

1 7/8"

DRAWER
GUIDE

19 3/4"
(PANEL)

SECTION B
(WITHOUT
DOORS AND DRAWERS)

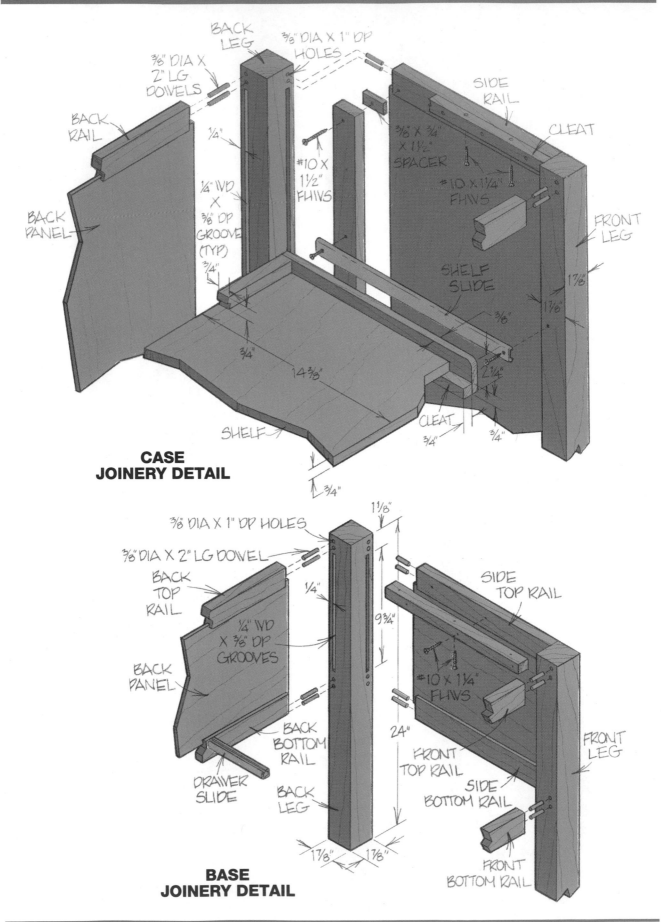

**CASE
JOINERY DETAIL**

**BASE
JOINERY DETAIL**

7 Cut the drawer, door, and shelf parts.

Measure the openings in the case and stand. If these have changed, adjust the dimensions of the drawer, door, and shelf parts accordingly. Figure the plywood door panels approximately ¹⁄₁₆″ undersize to allow for wood movement. Cut the parts to size.

Note: As drawn, the shelves are 1″ narrower than the opening in the case. This is because you must allow space on either side of each shelf to attach the slides. Most slides are ½″ thick, but not *all* of them. Check the thickness of the slides you've purchased before you cut the shelf parts.

8 Make and install the drawer.

The drawer sides and front are joined by half-blind dovetails, and the back fits into dadoes. The drawer bottom fits into grooves in the front and sides, as shown in the *Drawer Layout*. Cut the dovetails with a router and a dovetail template, and the dadoes and grooves with a table-mounted router or dado cutter.

Finish sand the drawer parts, then dry assemble the drawer. If the parts fit satisfactorily, reassemble the front, back, and sides with glue. Slide the bottom into place and attach it to the bottom edge of the back with

screws. Countersink the heads of these screws. Do *not* glue the bottom in its grooves.

Let the glue dry and sand all joints clean and flush. Attach the pull and test fit the drawer in the stand opening. Because you've cut the parts to the same size as this opening, the drawer will probably be too large to slide in and out smoothly. Sand or scrape the surfaces of the drawer until it fits properly.

Attach a metal slide to the bottom front and back rails, and a matching guide to the bottom of the drawer. Install the drawer in the stand, fitting the guide to the slide.

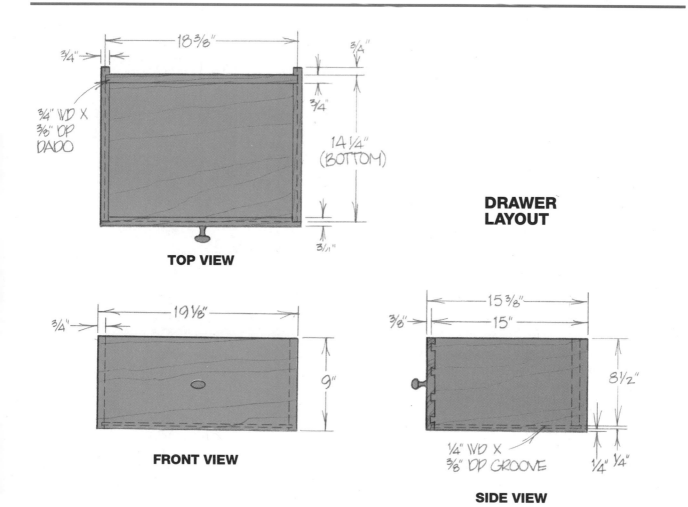

DRAWER LAYOUT

TOP VIEW

FRONT VIEW

SIDE VIEW

9

Make and install the shelves. Round the front top corners of the shelf sides, as shown in the *Shelf Layout/Side View*. Finish sand the shelf parts, then attach the three-hole cleats and shelf sides to the shelf bottoms, using flathead wood screws. Do *not* glue the cleats or the sides to the bottoms. However, attach the shelf back to the bottoms with glue. When the glue dries, sand all joints clean and flush.

The shelves are mounted on extension slides. Most of these slides separate into two pieces. Following the manufacturer's directions, take each slide apart, fasten one part to the inside of the case, and fasten the other to a shelf. To install the shelves, put the shelves in place, line up the tabs and slots in the slides, and snap the slide parts together again.

10

Make and install the doors. The slide-out shelves are hidden by two frame-and-panel doors. The rails and stiles of these doors are joined by tongues and grooves, and the door panels float in grooves. You can make these joints with a table-mounted router or a dado cutter.

Cut ¼"-wide, ⅜"-deep grooves in all the *inside* edges of the door rails and stiles. (See Figure 6.) Then cut matching tenons on the ends of the rails. (See Figure 7.)

Like the stand and case frames, the inside edges of the door frames are cut with decorative beads. Make these beads in the same manner that you cut the others. Dry assemble the frames, clamp them to the workbench, cut the beads, and square the corners. When you've finished, dismantle the frames.

Finish sand the door parts, then assemble the rails and stiles with glue. Slide the panels in place as you do so, but do *not* glue them in the grooves. Check that the doors are square when you clamp the parts together.

6/When making tongue-and-groove joints, always cut the grooves first, then fit the tongues to them. Using a router or dado cutter, cut grooves in the side edges of the frame members. These grooves must be **centered** in the edges.

7/To make the tenons, cut a rabbet in the ends of each rail, turn the board over, and cut another rabbet. Test fit the resulting tenon in a groove. If it's too tight, raise the bit or cutter. If it's too loose, lower it.

> **TRY THIS!** If the doors of this wardrobe will see heavy use, reinforce the tongue-and-groove joints with dowels. At each joint, drill one or two ⅜"-diameter, 2½"-deep holes through the stile and into the rail *after* the door frames are assembled. Apply a little glue inside the holes, then drive ⅜"-diameter, 2½"-long dowels into them. Sand the ends of the dowels flush with the surface.

Let the glue dry, and sand the joints clean and flush. Mortise the outside door stiles and front case stiles for hinges. Mount the hinges on the doors, then install the doors in the case. Also, install door pulls on the inside stiles, and bullet catches at the top and bottom inside corners of each door. (See Figure 8.)

8/To mount a bullet catch, drill a hole in the door frame and insert the barrel of the catch. Mortise the surface where the bullet rubs and install a latch.

11

Finish the wardrobe. Remove the doors, shelves, and drawer from the wardrobe. Also remove all the hardware and set it aside. Do any necessary touch-up sanding, then apply a finish to all wooden surfaces *except* the shelves and the drawer sides, back, and bottom. If you leave these parts raw, they will absorb moisture in humid weather. This, in turn, will help keep the fabric items you store in the wardrobe from mildewing.

Be careful to apply as many coats of finish to the *inside* of the stand and case as you do to the outside. This will ensure that all the parts absorb and release moisture at an even rate. As a result, the parts will be less likely to warp or bow, and the assembly will remain square.

When the finish dries, rub it out and buff it with paste wax. Assemble the case and stand. Replace the hardware, shelves, doors, and drawer.

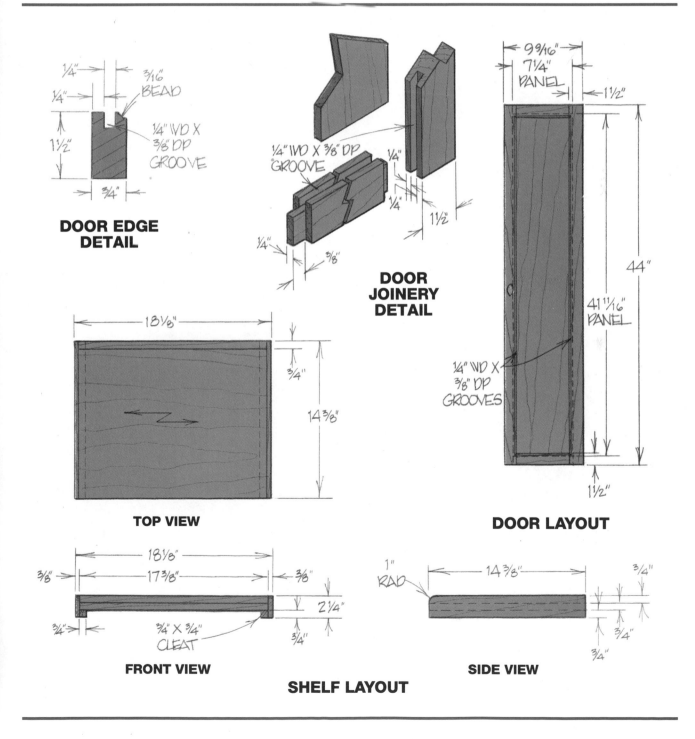

DOOR EDGE DETAIL

DOOR JOINERY DETAIL

TOP VIEW

DOOR LAYOUT

FRONT VIEW

SIDE VIEW

SHELF LAYOUT

Making and Using a Scratch Stock

Before there were power shapers, molders, and routers, craftsmen typically *scraped* small, decorative shapes into the wood. They used molding planes to cut large shapes, but found they could get better results by scraping small ones. To do this, they used a *scratch stock* or *beader* (so called because it was most often used to make beads). This simple hand tool was shaped like a spokeshave and held a small scraper blade nearly perpendicular to the wood surface. The end of the blade was ground to the shape that the craftsman wanted to make. (See Figure A.)

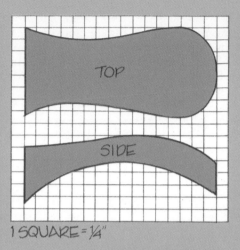

1 SQUARE = ¼"

HANDLE PATTERN

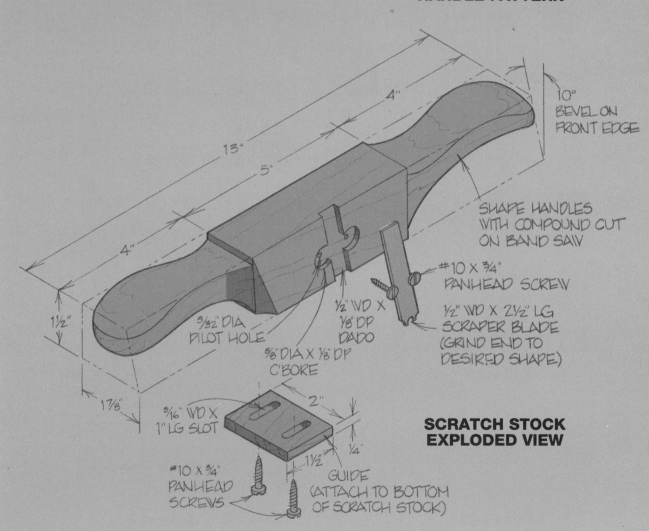

10°
BEVEL ON
FRONT EDGE

SHAPE HANDLES
WITH COMPOUND CUT
ON BAND SAW

#10 X ¾"
PANHEAD SCREW

½" WD X 2½" LG
SCRAPER BLADE
(GRIND END TO
DESIRED SHAPE)

13"

5"

4"

4"

1½"

1⅛"

5/32" DIA
PILOT HOLE

½" WD X
⅛" DP
DADO

⅝" DIA X ⅛" DP
C'BORE

3/16" WD X
1" LG SLOT

2"

¼"

1½"

#10 X ¾"
PANHEAD
SCREWS

GUIDE
(ATTACH TO BOTTOM
OF SCRATCH STOCK)

**SCRATCH STOCK
EXPLODED VIEW**

A scratch stock remains useful today. In many cases it will do a better job of cutting a small shape than a power tool. Because it scrapes rather than cuts, it doesn't lift the grain. Figured wood won't chip or splinter. And because it burnishes the surface as it scrapes, the completed shape requires little or no sanding.

You can make your own scratch stock from a 1½″ x 2″ x 13″ block of hardwood and an old scraper blade. Snip a ½″-wide, 2½″-long strip from the blade. Grind or file the shape you want to make in one end of the metal.

Bevel the front edge of the wooden block at 80°.

Rout or cut a ½″-wide, ⅛″-deep dado in the beveled edge to hold the blade. Drill counterbores and pilot holes on either side of the dado. Cut comfortable handles in the block, then fasten the blade to the block with two panhead screws. (See Figure B.)

To use the tool, draw it over the surface of the wood repeatedly, pressing down firmly. The blade should lean in the same direction that you draw the tool, like a cabinet scraper. (See Figure C.) With each pass, the scratch stock will scrape away a small amount of wood. Little by little, the shape will evolve. To guide the tool, clamp a fence to the workpiece or fasten a guide to the sole of the tool.

A/A scratch stock looks like a spokeshave, but works like a cabinet scraper. You can make your own from a block of hardwood and an old scraper blade.

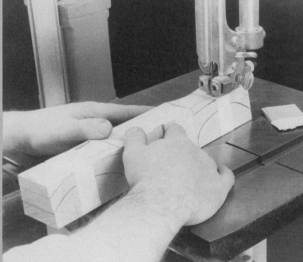

B/Shape the handles by making a compound cut on a band saw. Cut the side pattern first, tape the waste back to the block, and cut the top pattern. Discard the waste and the tape, and round the edges of the handles with a file or sandpaper.

C/Draw the scratch stock along the wood with the blade leaning in the same direction that the tool is moving. Make multiple passes until the shape is complete.

Photo Treasure Chest

While it's convenient to mount photos in an album, you may also want to pass them around among friends and family. This small chest offers a way to do both. It's designed to hold standard-size plastic sheets for mounting photos. But it holds them *loose* — un-bound — so you can easily pass them around when the occasion calls for it.

The chest is just a simple box, joined at the corners with dovetails. The top and bottom are flat panels. The lid is cut from the box in such a way that the sides are relieved. This makes it easier to remove and replace the plastic sheets.

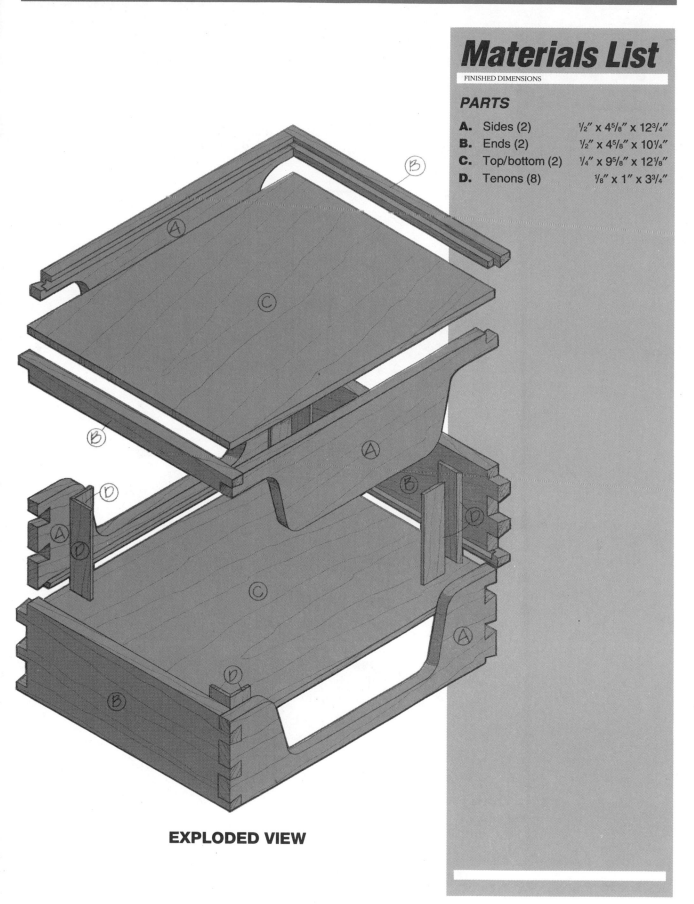

EXPLODED VIEW

Materials List

FINISHED DIMENSIONS

PARTS

A. Sides (2) $\frac{1}{2}$" x $4\frac{5}{8}$" x $12\frac{3}{4}$"
B. Ends (2) $\frac{1}{2}$" x $4\frac{5}{8}$" x $10\frac{1}{4}$"
C. Top/bottom (2) $\frac{1}{4}$" x $9\frac{5}{8}$" x $12\frac{1}{8}$"
D. Tenons (8) $\frac{1}{8}$" x 1" x $3\frac{3}{4}$"

1

Select the stock and cut the parts to size. To make this project, you need about 3 board feet of 4/4 (four-quarters) stock. You can use almost any cabinet-grade lumber, but since this will hold special memories, select special stock. On the chest shown, the sides and ends are made from curly maple, while the top and bottom are made from bird's-eye maple.

Plane 1½ board feet of the stock to ½″ thick and cut the sides and the ends to size. Resaw the remaining stock in half, plane it to ¼″ thick, and glue up the stock needed to make the wide top and bottom. Cut and plane all the remaining stock to ⅛″ thick and set it aside to make the tenons. *Don't* cut them yet. Wait until after you've assembled the chest.

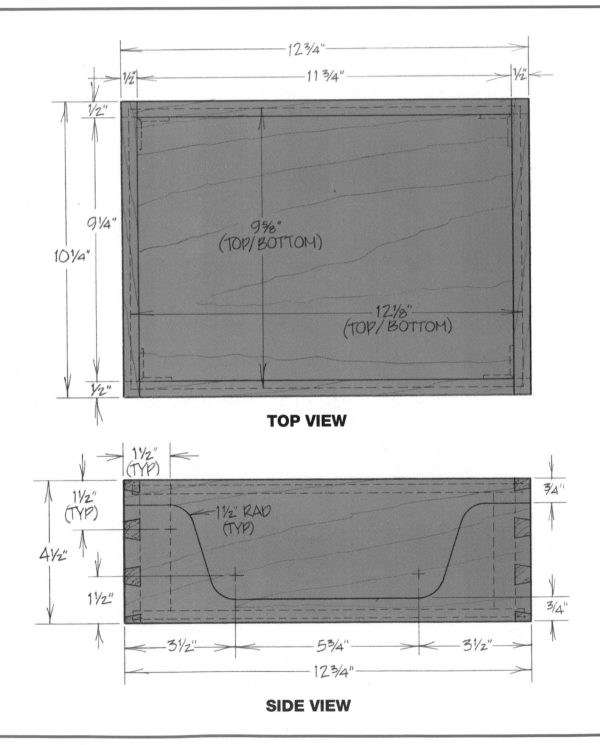

TOP VIEW

SIDE VIEW

2 Cut the blind grooves.

The bottom and the top are held by double-blind grooves (closed at both ends), as shown in the *Blind Groove Detail*. This prevents you from seeing the grooves on the assembled chest.

Cut all the grooves *before* you make the dovetails. If you have an overarm router, you'll find this is the best tool for the job. If you don't have one, make yourself an *Overhead Routing Jig*, as shown in the drawings — it's a good second-best. Mount a ¼" straight bit in the router and clamp a straightedge to the workbench to guide the workpieces. Carefully mark the blind ends of each groove on the stock. Turn on the router, lower the bit into the wood at one end of the groove, and cut until you reach the opposite end. (See Figure 1.)

When you finish routing the grooves, square the ends with a small chisel.

1/Use an overarm router or overhead routing jig to cut the blind grooves. This arrangement gives you a clear view of each groove as you cut it.

3 Cut the dovetails.

Carefully lay out the dovetails on the sides and ends. Don't worry if one or more of the dovetails is positioned so it will cut through a groove and open a blind end. This will make no difference after final assembly; the newly opened ends of the grooves will be hidden by the adjoining boards.

The dovetails, however, will show — on both the sides and the ends. You can make these joints, called *through dovetails*, by hand or with power tools. If you

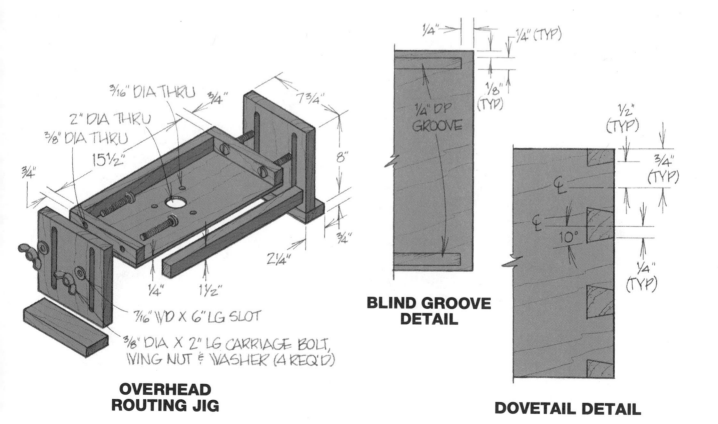

**OVERHEAD
ROUTING JIG**

**BLIND GROOVE
DETAIL**

DOVETAIL DETAIL

make them by hand, cut the pins first, using a fine saw and a chisel. Use the pins as a template to mark the tails, then cut the tails with the same tools.

If you make the dovetail joints with power tools, as shown, use a router and a dovetail jig. Two companies offer special jigs that will make through dovetails. These are available from most mail-order woodworking suppliers, or you can write:

Leigh Industries
P.O. Box 357
Port Coquitlam, BC
Canada V3C 4K6

Keller & Co.
1327 I Street
Petaluma, CA 94952

Both jigs work in a similar manner. A guide bushing mounted on the base of the router rides against the fingers of the jig. This controls the cut. You cut the tails using a dovetail router bit, and the pins using a straight bit. (See Figure 2.)

Most woodworkers prefer to make the parts of the joint in the opposite order that you would if you were doing them by hand — tails first, then pins. (It's much easier to fit the pins to the tails than it is the other way around.) As you rout, use a scrap block to back up the workpiece and to keep the wood from chipping and tearing. (See Figures 3 and 4.) If the joint doesn't fit correctly, adjust the jig as necessary. Dry assemble the routed parts to check the fit of the dovetail joints. If you've set up the router and the jig properly, you shouldn't have to do any handwork to adjust the fit. (See Figure 5.)

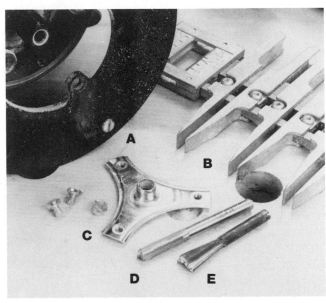

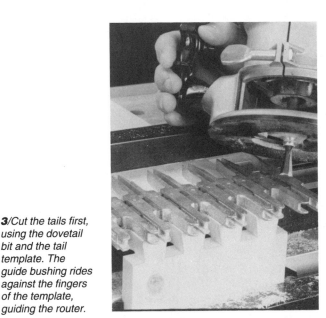

3/Cut the tails first, using the dovetail bit and the tail template. The guide bushing rides against the fingers of the template, guiding the router.

2/There are two router jigs that enable you to cut through dovetails. In addition to a router **(a)** and the jig **(b)**, you also need a guide bushing **(c)**, a straight bit **(d)**, and a dovetail bit **(e)**.

4/Change to the straight bit and the pin template. Rout the pins in the same manner that you cut the tails.

5/Fit the pins and tails together. If the fit is too tight or too loose, adjust the position of the pin template on the stock.

4 **Assemble the box.** Finish sand the *inside* surfaces of the sides and ends, and both surfaces of the top and bottom. Test fit the parts; they should fit snugly, but not too tightly. When you're satisfied with the fit, assemble the sides and ends with glue. Put the top and bottom in place, but do *not* glue them in the grooves. Let them float, so they can expand and contract with changes in temperature and humidity.

Check that the chest is square as you clamp the parts together. Wipe away any excess glue with a wet rag, then let the glue cure for at least 24 hours. Sand the joints clean and flush.

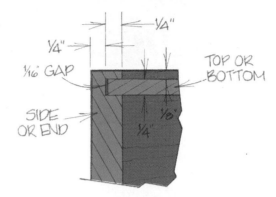

TOP AND BOTTOM JOINERY

5 **Cut the lid from the box.** Lay out the shape of the lid on both sides of the box, as shown in the *Side View*. If you have a band saw with a sufficient depth of cut (at least 10½"), use it to cut the lid free from the box. If you don't have access to a band saw with this capacity, cut the ends of the lid on a table saw, then cut the sides with a saber saw. (See Figure 6.) Sand the sawed edges.

6/To cut the lid free from the box, cut the straight ends on a table saw. Then cut the curved sides with a saber saw.

6 **Make and install the tenons.** To keep the lid from shifting on the chest, tenons protrude ³⁄₈" above each corner. Cut these tenons from ¹⁄₈"-thick stock and bevel the adjoining edges at 45°. Finish sand the tenons, then glue them in place in the corners of the box.

When the glue dries, round over the top edges of the tenons with sandpaper so the lid won't bind or hang up when you put it in place. Test the fit of the lid — it should fit snugly (but not too tightly) over the tenons, with no slop.

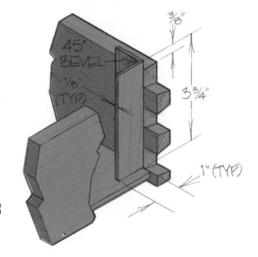

CORNER TENON DETAIL

7 **Finish the chest.** Finish sand the outside of the box, and apply a finish to all surfaces. Be sure to apply as many coats to the inside of the chest as to the outside. After the finish dries, wax and buff the chest. Allow the project to sit for several days with the lid off before you store photographs in it.

New England Mule Chest

Chests have been used for storage since Egyptian times. They remained fundamentally unchanged for thousands of years until the early sixteenth century, when European furnituremakers introduced an important innovation. To make it easier to reach items deep inside a chest, they raised the bottom and installed what was then called a "drawing box" beneath it. (The term "drawing box" was later shortened to "drawer.") These one-drawer chests were known as "mule chests."

The mule chest became increasingly popular in the seventeenth century on both sides of the Atlantic — in Europe and its American colonies. The piece shown is a copy of a New England country chest from the late seventeenth or early eighteenth century. Like most country furniture, it's simply made. The case is built from broad planks and nailed together. There are few joints and little decoration — although country craftsmen were often highly skilled, they tended to be short on time, tools, and money.

This reproduction was designed and built at the Workshops of David T. Smith, near Lebanon, Ohio. David and the craftsmen who work with him make American country pieces in the old tradition, and have published a book of their designs, *American Country Furniture*, available from Rodale Press.

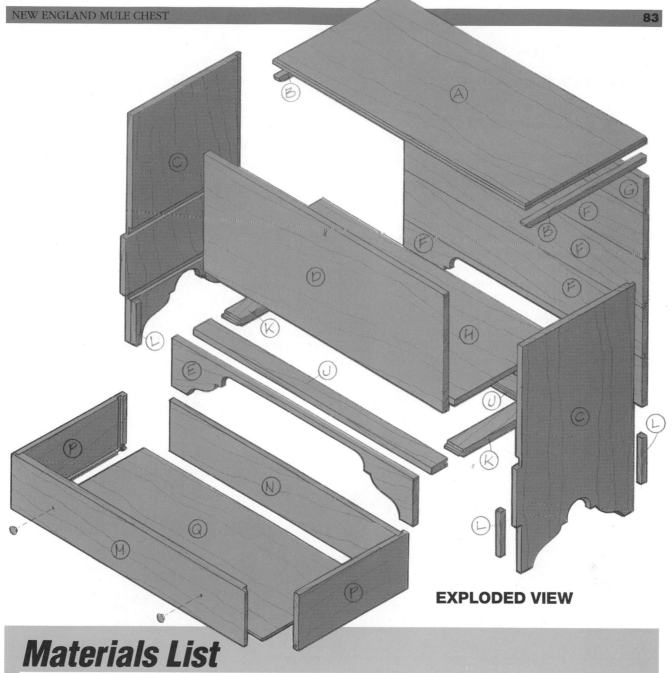

EXPLODED VIEW

Materials List

FINISHED DIMENSIONS

PARTS

A. Lid $3/4''$ x $19^3/4''$ x $41^9/16''$
B. Lid braces (2) $3/4''$ x $1''$ x $19^3/4''$
C. Sides (2) $3/4''$ x $19''$ x $32^1/4''$
D. Front $3/4''$ x $17''$ x $40''$
E. Front feet $3/4''$ x $7''$ x $40''$
F. Backboards (4) $3/4''$ x $7''$ x $39^1/4''$
G. Top backboard $3/4''$ x $5^3/4''$ x $39^1/4''$
H. Bottom $3/4''$ x $17^1/2''$ x $39^1/4''$

J. Web frame
     rails (2) $3/4''$ x $2^1/2''$ x $39^1/4''$
K. Web frame
     stiles (2) $3/4''$ x $2^1/2''$ x $13''$
L. Glue blocks (4) $3/4''$ x $3/4''$ x $6^1/4''$
M. Drawer front $3/4''$ x $8^3/16''$ x $38^7/16''$
N. Drawer back $1/2''$ x $7^{11}/16''$ x $37^{15}/16''$
P. Drawer sides (2) $1/2''$ x $8^3/16''$ x $18''$
Q. Drawer
     bottom $1/2''$ x $17^1/4''$ x $37^{15}/16''$

HARDWARE

$1^1/2''$ x $3''$ Butt hinges and mounting
   screws (2)
Chest lock, latch, and mounting
   screws
$2''$-dia. Wooden drawer pulls (2)
4d Square-shanked cut nails ($1/4$ lb.)
6d Square-shanked cut nails ($1/4$ lb.)
#8 x $1^1/4''$ Flathead wood screws (3)

1

Select the stock and cut the parts to size. To make this project, you need about 55 board feet of 4/4 (four-quarters) stock. You can use almost any cabinet-grade wood, but old-time country craftsmen typically built chests such as these from soft, easy-to-work woods such as white pine, cedar, cypress, and poplar. The chest shown is made from poplar.

When you have selected the wood, plane all the stock to ³/₄″ thick. Glue up the boards needed to make the wide parts — lid, sides, front, and bottom. Cut all the parts to size *except* the drawer parts; lay stock aside for these.

2

Cut the joinery in the sides, backboards, and web frame members. The parts of the case are joined with simple rabbets, dadoes, and grooves. Make these joints with a dado cutter or router:

- ³/₄″-wide, ³/₈″-deep dadoes in the sides to hold the bottom and the web frame, as shown in the *Side Layout*
- ³/₄″-wide, ³/₈″-deep rabbets in the sides to hold the backboards
- ³/₈″-wide, ³/₈″-deep rabbets in the adjoining edges of the backboards, as shown in the *Backboard Joinery Detail*

- ¹/₄″-wide, ¹/₄″-deep grooves in the inside edges of the web frame rails, as shown in the *Web Frame Layout*

Also cut ¹/₄″-thick, ¹/₄″-long tenons in the ends of the web frame stiles to fit the grooves in the web frame rails. To make these tenons, cut ¹/₄″-wide, ¹/₄″-deep rabbets on each end of the boards. Turn the boards over and cut matching rabbets on the opposite faces. Each pair of rabbets will form a tenon. (See Figures 1 and 2.)

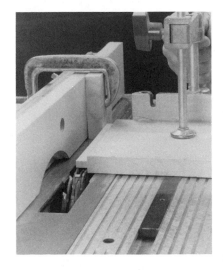

*1/To make the web frame, first cut ¹/₄″-wide, ¹/₄″-deep grooves in the **inside** edges of the rails, using a dado cutter or table-mounted router.*

2/With the same tool, cut matching tenons in the ends of the stiles.

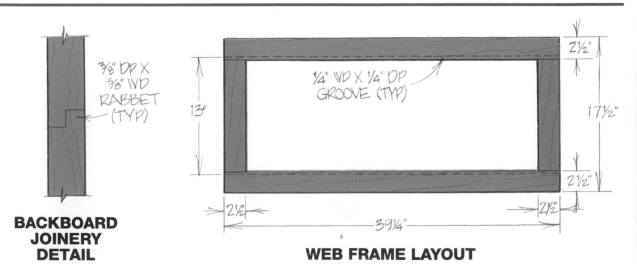

BACKBOARD JOINERY DETAIL

³/₈″ DP X ³/₈″ WD RABBET (TYP)

WEB FRAME LAYOUT

¹/₄″ WD X ¹/₄″ DP GROOVE (TYP)

2½″

13″

17½″

2½″

2½″

2½″

39¼″

3 *Cut the shapes of the sides and feet.*

Enlarge the *Foot Pattern* and lay out the feet on the sides, bottom backboard, and front feet stock. Also lay out the notches in the front edges of the sides, as shown in the *Side Layout*. Cut the feet and notches with a band saw or saber saw. Sand the sawed edges.

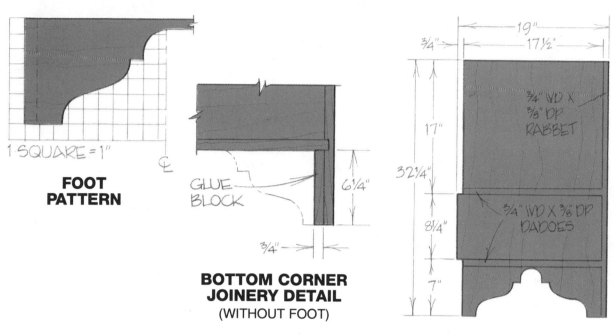

1 SQUARE = 1"

FOOT PATTERN

BOTTOM CORNER JOINERY DETAIL
(WITHOUT FOOT)

GLUE BLOCK

6¼"

¾"

SIDE LAYOUT

19"

17½"

¾"

17"

¾" WD X ⅜" DP RABBET

32¼"

¾" WD X ⅜" DP DADOES

8¼"

7"

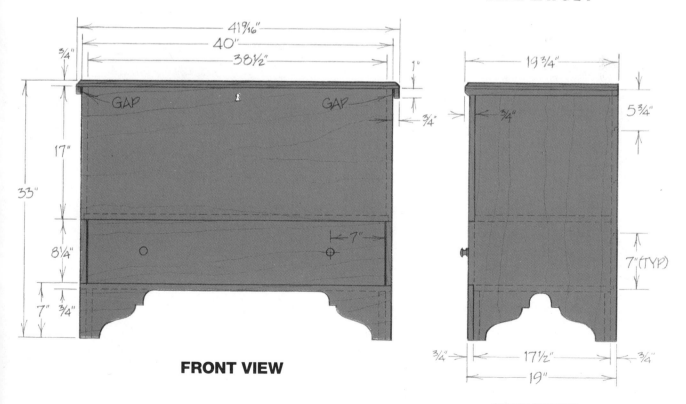

FRONT VIEW

41 9/16"

40"

38½"

¾"

GAP   GAP

1"

¾"

17"

33"

8¼"

7"   ¾"

7"

SIDE VIEW

19¾"

¾"

5¾"

7" (TYP)

¾"   17½"   ¾"

19"

4 **Assemble the chest.** Mortise the inside face of the front for the chest lock, and cut a keyhole. Finish sand all the parts of the chest that you've made, except the glue blocks. Stain the rabbeted edges of the backboards a dark brown or black, and scrape off any stain that bleeds over on the faces. This stain helps to disguise the cracks that appear between the backboards when the wood shrinks during the dry time of the year.

Glue the web frame members together, then glue the web frame and bottom to the sides. Reinforce the glue joints with 4d square-shanked cut nails. Drill $^5/_{32}''$-diameter pilot holes for the nails, then drive them through the sides and into the bottom and web frame. (See Figure 3.)

Note: You *must* drill pilot holes for cut nails, especially when installing them in soft or brittle woods. The nails act like tiny wedges and can split the wood. Refer to Using Square-Cut Nails on page 88.

Join the backboards to the sides with 4d cut nails, driving the nails through the sides and into the ends of the backboards. Join the front to the sides with 6d cut nails — drill $^3/_{16}''$-diameter pilot holes and drive the nails through the front and into the edges of the sides. Glue the top and bottom backboards, but *not* the chest front or the middle backboards. If you do, the glue will

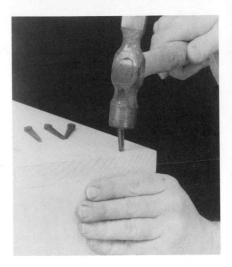

3/Use square-shanked cut nails to assemble the mule chest. These nails imitate the look of old-time hand-forged nails.

prevent the parts from moving properly with changes in temperature and humidity, and the chest will eventually warp or split. When you assemble these parts with nails only, the nails will flex slightly as the parts expand and contract, and the chest will remain square.

Glue the front feet to the sides and reinforce the joints with 6d nails. Then glue the glue blocks to the sides, front feet, and bottom backboard.

When the glue dries, set the heads of all the nails. Sand all the joints clean and flush.

5 **Chamfer the lid and lid braces.** Using a table saw or a plane, cut 45° chamfers in the top front and side edges of the lid, as shown in the *Lid/ Brace Profile*. (See Figure 4.) Also round the front bottom corners of the lid braces.

4/Use a hollow-ground planer blade to cut the chamfers in the lid — this type of blade leaves a very smooth cut that requires little sanding.

6 **Assemble and install the lid.** Position the lid on the chest, then clamp the braces to it. There should be about $^1/_{32}''$–$^1/_{16}''$ clearance between the outside faces of the sides and the inside faces of the braces. Remove the lid from the chest and fasten the lid braces to the lid with 4d cut nails. Drive the nails down through the lid and into the braces, and set the heads. Do *not* glue the braces to the lid.

Mortise the top edge of the top backboard and the bottom face of the lid for hinges. Attach the hinges to the lid, then mount the lid on the chest.

Install the lock in the chest front, and insert the latch in the lock. Close the lid and press down hard enough for the latch plate to make an impression on the bottom face of the lid. Using this impression as a guide, mortise the lid for the latch and install it.

7 Cut the drawer parts and joinery.

Measure the drawer opening in the assembled chest. If the dimensions of the opening have changed from what is shown in the drawings, adjust the size of the drawer parts accordingly and cut them out. Plane the remaining ³/₄″-thick stock to ½″, and glue up the boards needed to make the wide drawer bottom. Cut the drawer sides, back, and bottom to size.

Like the chest, the drawer is assembled with simple rabbets, dadoes, and grooves. Cut the following joints:

■ ½″-wide, ½″-deep rabbets in the ends of the drawer front to hold the sides, as shown in the *Drawer/Top View*

■ ½″-wide, ¼″-deep dadoes in the drawer sides to hold the back

■ ¼″-wide, ¼″-deep grooves in the drawer front and sides to hold the bottom, as shown in the *Drawer Bottom Detail*

Chamfer the front and side edges of the drawer bottom with a table saw or hand plane so that it will fit the ¼″-wide grooves in the drawer parts.

TRY THIS! Many cabinetmakers make drawer parts slightly oversize, then sand them to the proper dimensions after the case and the drawers are assembled. This way they get a perfect fit.

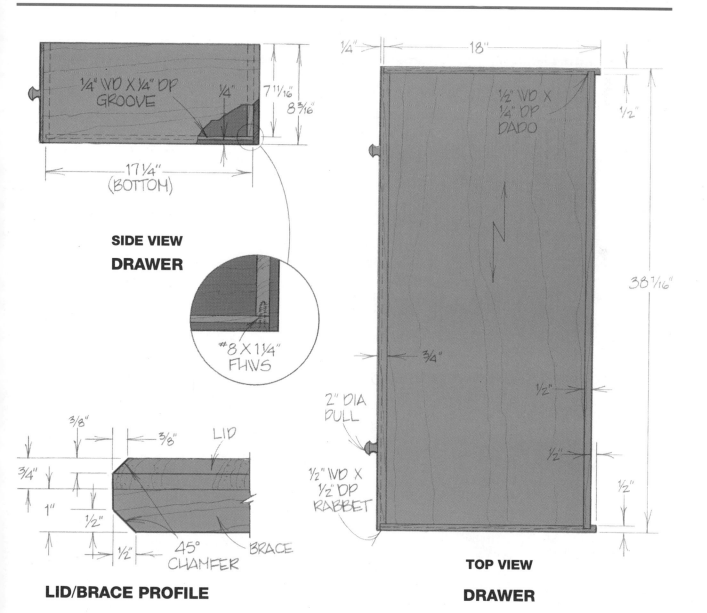

1/4" WO X 1/4" DP GROOVE   1/4"   7 11/16"   8 3/16"

17 1/4" (BOTTOM)

SIDE VIEW
DRAWER

#8 X 1 1/4" FHWS

1/4"   18"   1/2"

1/2" WO X 1/4" DP DADO

38 7/16"

3/4"

2" DIA PULL

1/2"

1/2" WO X 1/2" DP RABBET

1/2"

TOP VIEW
DRAWER

3/8"   3/8"   LID

3/4"   1"   1/2"

1/2"   45° CHAMFER   BRACE

LID/BRACE PROFILE

8

Assemble and fit the drawer. Finish sand the drawer front, and lightly sand the other parts. Glue the front, sides, and back together, and reinforce the joints with 4d cut nails. Slide the bottom into its grooves, and fasten it to the back with #8 x 1¼″ flathead wood screws. Countersink the heads of the screws. Do *not* glue the bottom in the grooves; let it float. When the glue dries, sand the joints clean and flush, then install pulls on the drawer front.

Test the fit of the drawer in the opening. It should slide in and out easily. When you slide it all the way in so the sides butt against the backboards, the drawer front should be flush with the front of the chest. If the drawer is too tight or it protrudes, sand or scrape stock from the drawer surfaces until it fits properly.

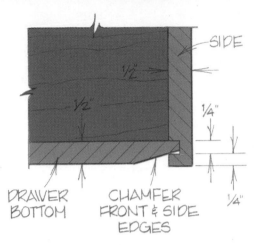

DRAWER BOTTOM DETAIL

9

Finish the chest. Remove the drawer and the lid from the chest. Also remove the hinges and lock and set them aside. Do any necessary touch-up sanding, then apply a finish to all wooden surfaces. When the finish dries, reassemble the chest.

Using Square-Cut Nails

Many old-time chests and boxes were assembled with nails. Craftsmen often didn't have the time, tools, or expertise to make fancy joinery, so they used nails. These nails, however, were very different from modern nails: They were hand forged, with square shanks and heads.

If you want to imitate the look of these old nails, you can use *square-cut nails* (or simply "cut nails"), which are still available in most hardware stores. (See Figure A.) Or you can purchase reproductions of hand-forged nails from:

Tremont Nail Company
8 Elm Street
P.O. Box 111
Wareham, MA 02571

Whether you use store-bought cut nails or hand-forged nails, you can't simply drive them into a board (particularly a hardwood board), because the nails act like tiny wedges and split the wood. Instead, drill pilot holes. Hammer the nails into the holes until ¹⁄₁₆″ –¹⁄₈″ protrudes from the surface, then set the heads with a punch. If the nails are rectangular rather than truly square, make sure the widest part of the shank is parallel with the wood grain.

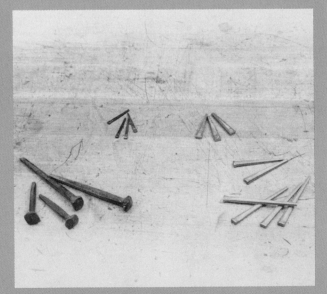

A/Tremont offers several different sizes and styles of hand-forged nails, including a fine-finishing nail.

Pantry Wall

Do you need more storage space in the kitchen, but lack the room for another full-size cupboard or shelving unit? Perhaps this pantry wall is the answer to your dilemma.

It's a shallow cabinet, just 8″ deep, that stretches floor to ceiling. It doesn't stand out far enough from the wall to block an entrance way, restrict traffic, or seriously diminish the floor space in your kitchen. Yet the pantry wall provides a great deal of storage. Despite its lack of depth, there is room on each shelf for one or two rows of canned goods. It will also hold mops and brooms, a fold-out ironing board, and dozens of other small- and medium-size domestic items.

Larry Callahan designed this storage system to be easy and inexpensive to build. Because the unit is attached to the wall, it requires few structural members and only basic joinery. Furthermore, the design can be easily adapted to many different kitchens. Depending on the space available, it can be expanded to fill an entire wall, or diminished to cover just a portion. ✱

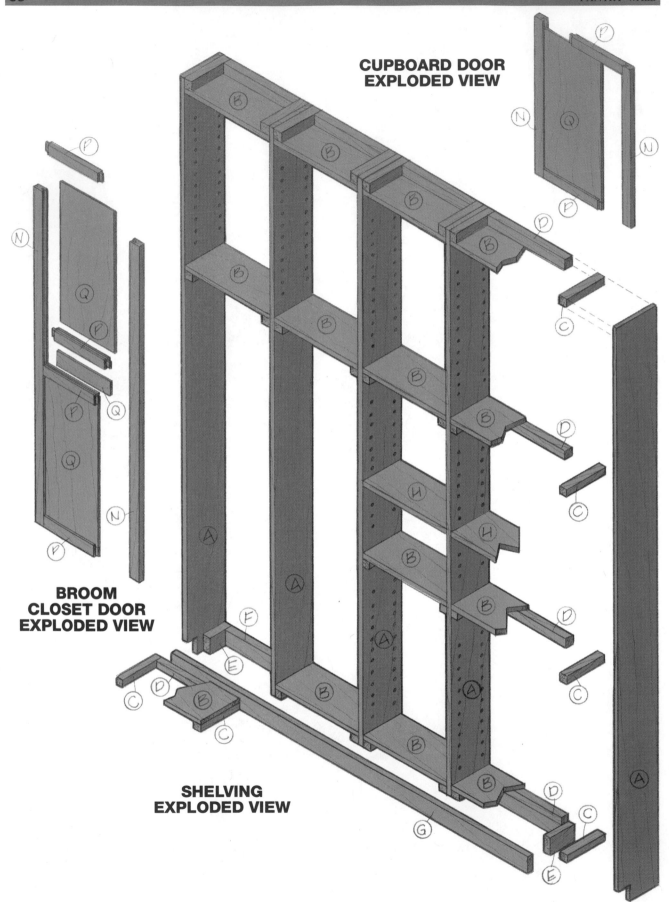

**CUPBOARD DOOR
EXPLODED VIEW**

**BROOM
CLOSET DOOR
EXPLODED VIEW**

**SHELVING
EXPLODED VIEW**

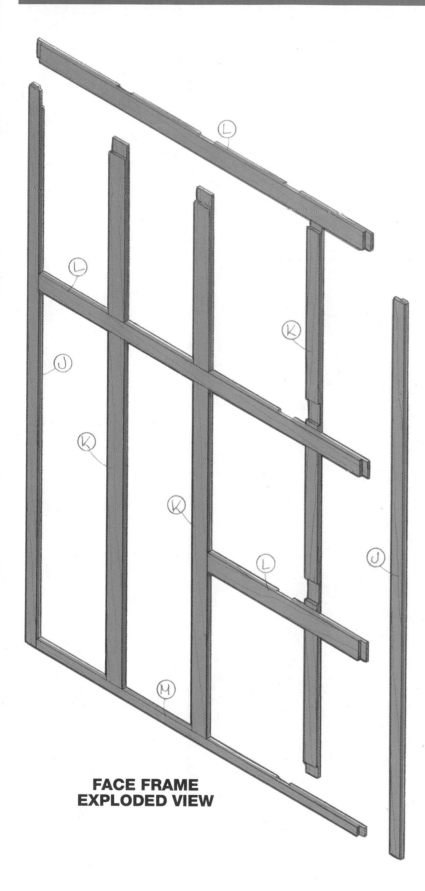

**FACE FRAME
EXPLODED VIEW**

Materials List

FINISHED DIMENSIONS

PARTS

A. Shelving supports
(2 or more) $^3/_4$" x 8" x (variable)

B. Fixed shelves $^3/_4$" x 8" x
(2 or more) ($13^3/_4$"–$19^3/_4$")

C. Top/middle cleats
(4 or more) $1^1/_2$" x $1^1/_2$" x 8"

D. Top/middle ledgers $1^1/_2$" x $1^1/_2$" x
(2 or more) ($10^3/_4$"–$16^3/_4$")

E. Bottom cleats
(2 or more) $1^1/_2$" x 3" x $4^1/_4$"

F. Bottom ledgers $1^1/_2$" x 3" x
(1 or more) ($10^3/_4$"–$16^3/_4$")

G. Toeboard $^3/_4$" x 3" x (variable)

H. Adjustable shelves $^3/_4$" x $7^7/_8$" x
(1 or more) ($13^5/_8$"–$19^5/_8$")

J. Outside face frame
stiles (2) $^3/_4$" x 2" x (variable)

K. Middle face frame stiles
(0 or more) $^3/_4$" x $3^1/_4$" x (variable)

L. Top/middle face frame rails
(1 or more) $^3/_4$" x $3^1/_4$" x (variable)

M. Bottom face
frame rail $^3/_4$" x $2^1/_4$" x (variable)

N. Door stiles $^3/_4$" x 2" x
(2 or more) (24"–$62^1/_2$")

P. Door rails
(2 or more) $^3/_4$" x 2" x (9"–15")

Q. Door panels $^1/_4$" x (9"–15") x
(1 or more) ($3^1/_2$"–27")

HARDWARE

$1^1/_2$"-dia. Door pulls (1 or more)
Offset self-closing cabinet door hinges
and mounting screws (2 or more)
#10 x $1^1/_2$" Flathead wood screws
(18 or more)
4d Finishing nails ($^1/_4$ lb. or more)
8d Finishing nails ($^1/_4$ lb. or more)
16d Common nails ($^1/_4$ lb. or more)

1

Determine the size and the configuration of the pantry wall. As Larry designed this project, there are just two sizes of compartments — a tall, narrow broom closet for brooms and mops, and a shorter cupboard for canned goods and other small items. These small compartments are fitted with adjustable shelves. By planning as many same-size compartments as possible, you can cut down on the number of parts you have to make. The adjustable shelves allow you to customize the storage space in each compartment.

Measure the wall space where you want to install this project, then give some thought to the size and arrangement of the compartments. Sketch a front view of the pantry wall you wish to build, and calculate the materials you need to build it. This sketch doesn't have to be as detailed as the drawings in this chapter, but it should provide adequate information to estimate the materials, cut the parts to size, and make the joinery.

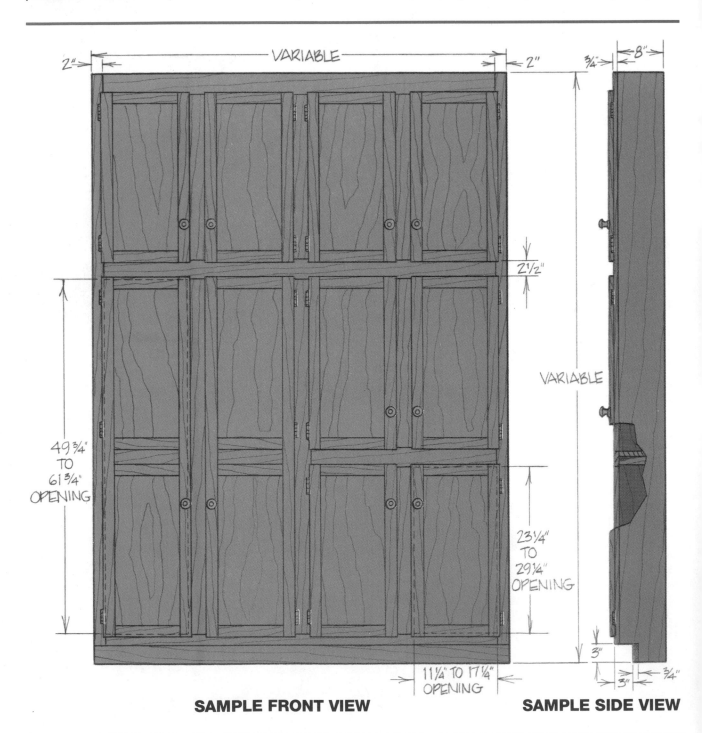

SAMPLE FRONT VIEW   **SAMPLE SIDE VIEW**

2 Select the stock and cut the parts to size.

To make this project, you need 4/4 (four-quarters) stock, ¼" plywood, and clear 2 x 4s. The amount of materials will vary according to the size of the pantry wall you wish to make and the number of compartments in it. All the materials should be cabinet-grade lumber, and the plywood veneer should match the 4/4 stock. The pantry wall shown is made from birch and birch-veneer plywood.

When you have gathered the materials, plane the 4/4 stock to ¾" thick. Cut the shelving supports and the shelves, then set the remaining stock aside for now — do *not* cut the toeboard, face frame, or door parts until you've built and installed the shelving.

Cut the bottom cleats and ledgers to size from the 2 x 4 stock. Rip the remaining 2 x 4s into 2 x 2s, exactly 1½" square. Cut the top and middle cleats and ledgers from the 2 x 2s.

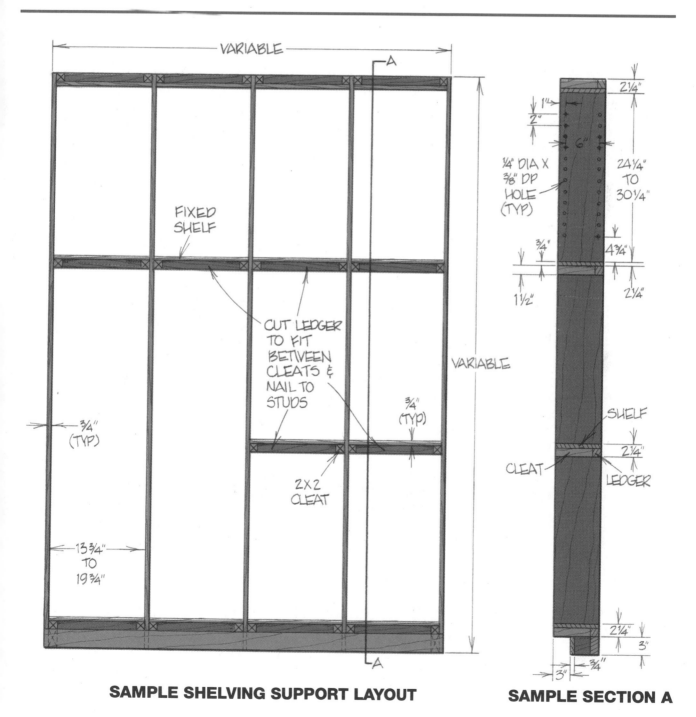

SAMPLE SHELVING SUPPORT LAYOUT   **SAMPLE SECTION A**

3 Drill holes in the shelving supports.

The adjustable shelves are held up by pin-style supports, which fit into ¼″-diameter, ⅜″-deep holes in the vertical shelving supports. Carefully lay out the location of these holes on each support, along with the locations of the cleats and ledgers, as shown in *Sample Section A*. Bore the holes with a hand drill or a drill press. If you're using a hand drill, attach a stop collar to the drill bit to ensure that all the holes are the same depth.

TRY THIS! If you don't want to drill dozens of holes, you can attach metal shelving standards to the inside surfaces of the shelving supports. Use clips that fit in the standards to support the adjustable shelves.

4 Attach the cleats and shelves to the supports.

The fixed shelves are held in place by cleats. Attach these cleats to the supports with glue and 8d finishing nails. Set the heads of the nails. Let the glue dry for at least 24 hours.

Remove the baseboards and other fixtures from the wall that might interfere with the installation of the shelves. Also, find and mark the location of the studs in the wall.

With a helper, stand the supports in place and attach the shelves to them with glue and 4d finishing nails. Set the heads of the nails.

5 Attach the shelves to the wall.

The shelving unit is held to the wall by the ledgers. To make sure that you install these ledgers in precisely the proper positions, first slide the shelving assembly into place and brace it so it's square. Fit the ledgers between the cleats and attach them to the wall with 16d nails, driving the nails through the ledgers and into the wall studs.

Fasten the back edges of the shelves to the ledgers with flathead wood screws. Countersink the heads of these screws, but don't cover the heads. Leave them accessible so you can easily remove the pantry wall should you ever need to.

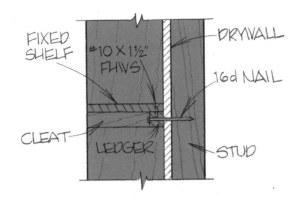

LEDGER-TO-WALL JOINERY DETAIL

TRY THIS! If you're attaching the ledgers to a masonry wall, use lag screws and expandable lead anchors. If you're attaching them to a portion of the wall where there are no studs, use Molly anchors or toggle bolts.

6 Make the face frame.

Measure the installed shelving unit and compare the actual dimensions of the assembly to those on your sketch. If they've changed significantly, you may have to adjust the sizes and positions of the face frame members. This is common for built-in projects, particularly if you're installing the pantry wall in an older house where the walls may not be precisely square or plumb.

Cut the face frame rails, stiles, and toeboard from ¾″-thick stock. These frame members are assembled in a grid with lap and half-lap joints, as shown in the *Sample Face Frame Layout* and *Face Frame Joinery Detail/ Back View*. Lay out the locations of these lap joints on the rails and stiles. As you do so, remember that when you attach the assembled face frame to the shelving unit, the top edges of the bottom and middle rails should be flush with the top surfaces of the fixed doors.

Cut the lap joints and half-lap joints with a dado cutter or hand-held router. If you use a router, make a simple jig to guide it, as shown in the *Lap-Joint Routing Jig* drawings. Square the corners of the half-lap with a chisel. (See Figures 1, 2, and 3.)

Dry assemble parts of the frame to test the fit of the lap joints. When you're satisfied the joints fit properly,

finish sand the inside edges of the frame members. Assemble the frame with glue, using a wet rag to wipe away any excess glue that squeezes out of the joints.

Clamp up the frame loosely, then tack it to the shelving unit with 4d finishing nails. Don't drive the nails all the way home; you'll need to remove them later. Make sure all the edges and surfaces that should be flush *are* flush, then tighten the clamps completely.

Let the glue dry at least 24 hours, then remove the clamps and the nails. Sand the lap joints clean and flush.

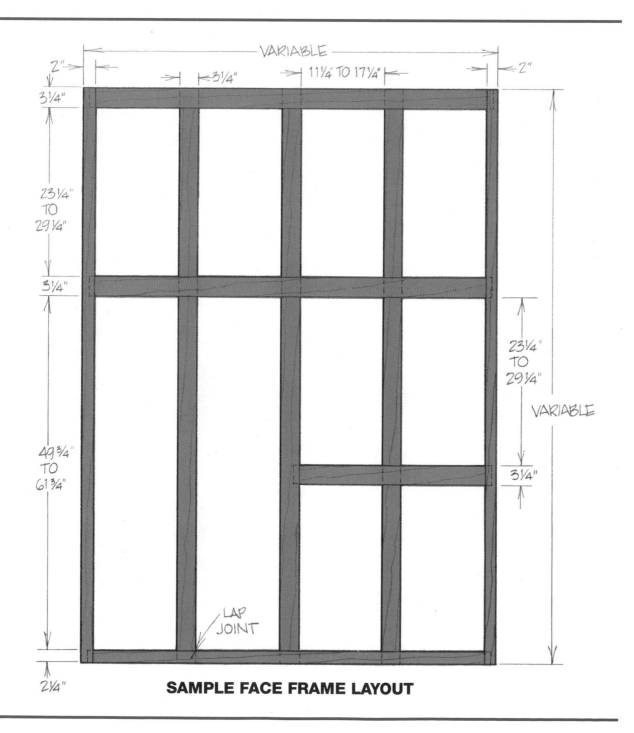

SAMPLE FACE FRAME LAYOUT

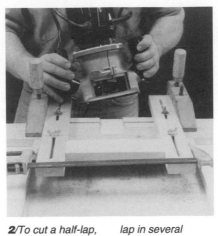

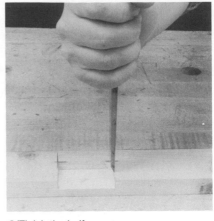

1/The lap-joint jig guides the router when cutting the recesses for each lap. Adjust the stretchers so they fit snugly over the stock, center the guides on either side of the layout lines, then clamp the jig to the stock. Cut the lap in several passes, cutting just ⅛"–¼" deeper with each cut.

2/To cut a half-lap, clamp a stop to one of the jig stretchers. Position the stop to halt the router so you only cut half-way across the stock, edge to edge. Cut the half- lap in several passes, as you did before.

3/Finish the half-lap by squaring the corners with a chisel.

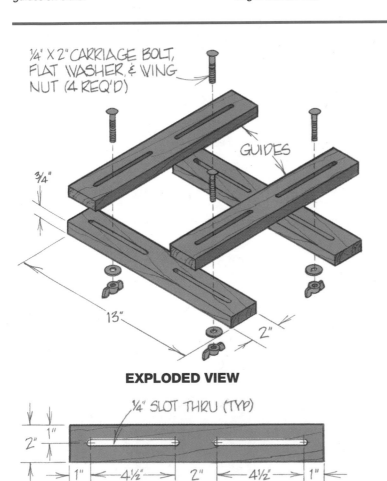

¼" X 2" CARRIAGE BOLT, FLAT WASHER, & WING NUT (4 REQ'D)

GUIDES

¾"

13"

2"

EXPLODED VIEW

¼" SLOT THRU (TYP)

2" 1"

1"   4½"   2"   4½"   1"

13"

GUIDE/TOP VIEW

LAP-JOINT ROUTING JIG

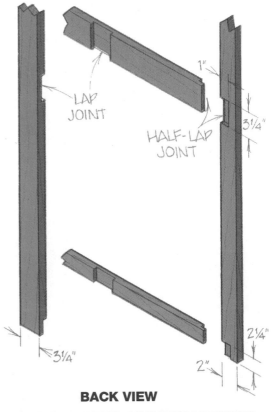

LAP JOINT

1"

HALF-LAP JOINT

3¼"

3¼"

2¼"

2"

BACK VIEW

FACE FRAME JOINERY DETAIL

7

Attach the face frame and toeboard to the shelving unit. Finish sand the toeboard. Spread glue on the front edges of the shelving unit, then attach the face frame and the toeboard with 4d finishing nails. Set the heads of the nails and cover them with wood putty. Finish sand the outside surface of the face frame.

8

Make the doors. Measure the openings in the face frame and compare the actual sizes to those on your sketch. Once again, they may have changed as you assembled the project. If so, adjust the lengths of the door frame members accordingly. Remember, each door should overlap its opening ³⁄₈″ on all four sides. Cut the door frame members from ³⁄₄″-thick stock, and the panels from ¹⁄₄″ plywood.

Using a dado cutter or table-mounted router, cut ¹⁄₄″-wide, ¹⁄₂″-deep grooves in all the *inside* edges of the door frame rails and stiles. Then cut ¹⁄₄″-thick, ¹⁄₂″-long tenons on the ends of the door rails using the same tool. The tenons on the rails should fit the grooves in the stiles, as shown in the *Door Joinery Detail.*

Dry assemble the doors to check the fit of the joints. When you're satisfied with the way in which they go together, finish sand the panels and the inside edges of the frame members. Reassemble the rails and stiles with glue, sliding the panels in place as you do so. Do *not* glue the panels in the grooves; let them float.

Let the glue dry, then sand the joints clean and flush.

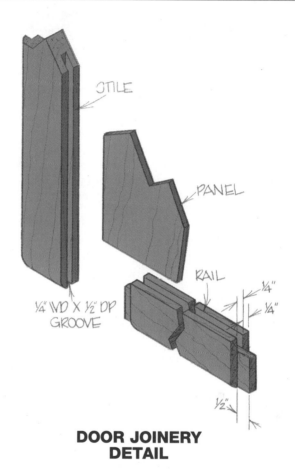

DOOR JOINERY DETAIL

9

Cut the lips in the doors. The doors are lipped — rabbeted all the way around the perimeter. The shoulders of these rabbets sit inside the door opening, and the lips cover it.

Before making the lips, you may wish to round over the outside ends and edges of each door with a router and a ³⁄₈″ quarter-round bit. (This is optional. Larry left the lips of his doors square.) Then cut ¹⁄₂″-wide, ³⁄₈″-deep rabbets in the inside ends and edges of the doors, as shown in the *Cabinet Door Lip Profile.*

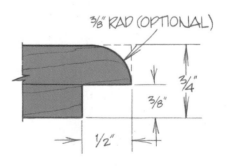

CABINET DOOR LIP PROFILE

10 **Mount the doors on the pantry wall.** Finish sand the surfaces of the doors that still need it. Then fasten the doors to the face frame with self-closing offset hinges. Install a pull on each door.

TRY THIS! You may wish to mount self-adhering rubber or felt pads to the back surfaces of the door lips where they strike the face frame. These will help muffle the sound when the doors close, and will keep the frame from being dented. The pads are available from the same sources that sell self-closing hinges. Some manufacturers include them with the hinges.

11 **Finish the pantry wall.** Remove the doors from the pantry wall and the hardware from the doors. Do any necessary touch-up sanding on the pantry wall and doors. Apply a finish or paint to all outside surfaces of the pantry, and all surfaces (front *and* back) of the doors. When the finish dries, rub it out if necessary. Apply a coat of paste wax to the finished surfaces and buff.

Install the adjustable shelves inside the pantry. If you wish, attach metal hangers for brooms and mops inside the larger compartments. Finally, replace the doors on the pantry wall.

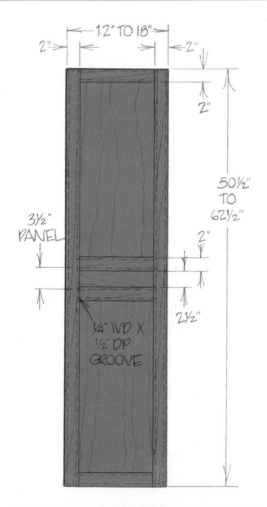

BROOM CLOSET DOOR LAYOUT

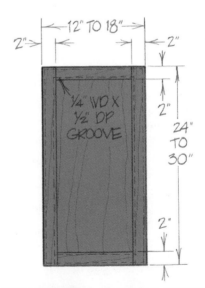

CUPBOARD DOOR LAYOUT

Herringbone Box

Making a herring-bone panel is an uncomplicated procedure. Simply glue up layers of contrasting wood, then cut them diagonally into strips. Glue the strips edge to edge so the grain seems to zigzag across them. These zigzags will form a distinctive herringbone pattern.

On the box shown, the herringbone panel is made from ordinary 3/4" plywood. By using plywood, you can make an intricate pattern in very little time — much of the gluing-up is already done.

The box itself is equally simple. All the parts are assembled with interlocking rabbets, dadoes, and grooves. Although the box looks fancy, the uncomplicated joinery makes it possible to build this project in a few evenings. ●

Materials List

FINISHED DIMENSIONS

PARTS

A. Front/back (2)   ½" x 3⅞" x 11"
B. Sides (2)   ½" x 3⅞" x 7½"
C. Bottom*   ½" x 7½" x 10½"
D. Top backing*   ¼" x 7½" x 10½"
E. Herringbone panel* ¼" x 7" x 10"

Make these parts from plywood.

HARDWARE

1½" x 2" Butt hinges and mounting
  screws (2)
Lid support and mounting screws
  (optional)

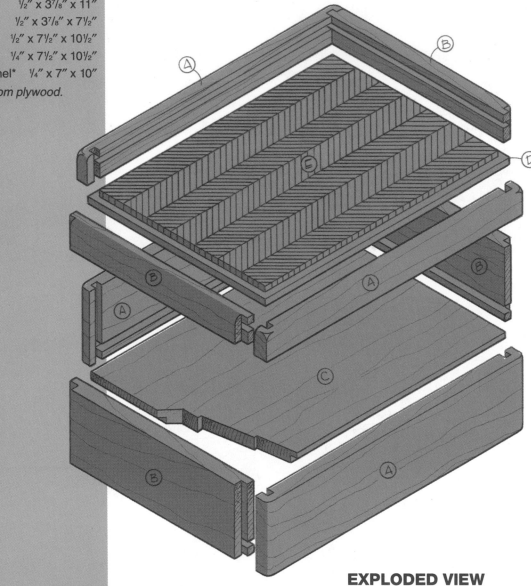

EXPLODED VIEW

1

Select the stock and cut the parts to size. To make this project, you need about 2 board feet of 4/4 (four-quarters) stock, a 10″ x 32″ scrap of ³/₄″ plywood, an 8″ x 11″ scrap of ¹/₂″ plywood, and an 8″ x 11″ scrap of ¹/₄″ plywood. As long as you use cabinet-grade wood and plywood, you can choose any kind or species of wood you want. (This is a good scrap-wood project.) On the box shown, the front and sides are cherry. The plywood is oak veneer with a mahogany core.

When you have selected the materials, plane the 4/4 stock to ¹/₂″ thick. Cut the parts to the sizes specified in the Materials List, *except* the plywood for the herringbone panel.

2

Cut the box joinery. As mentioned previously, the parts of the box are joined with interlocking rabbets, dadoes, and grooves. Make these joints with a dado cutter or a table-mounted router:

- ¹/₄″-wide, ¹/₄″-deep rabbets in the ends of the sides
- a ¹/₄″-wide, ¹/₄″-deep rabbet all around the perimeter of the bottom
- ¹/₄″-wide, ¹/₄″-deep dadoes, ¹/₄″ from the ends of the front and back
- ¹/₄″-wide, ¹/₄″-deep grooves, ¹/₄″ from the top and bottom edges of the front, back, and sides

Dry assemble the front, back, sides, bottom, and top backing to check the fit of the joints. Clamp the parts together temporarily.

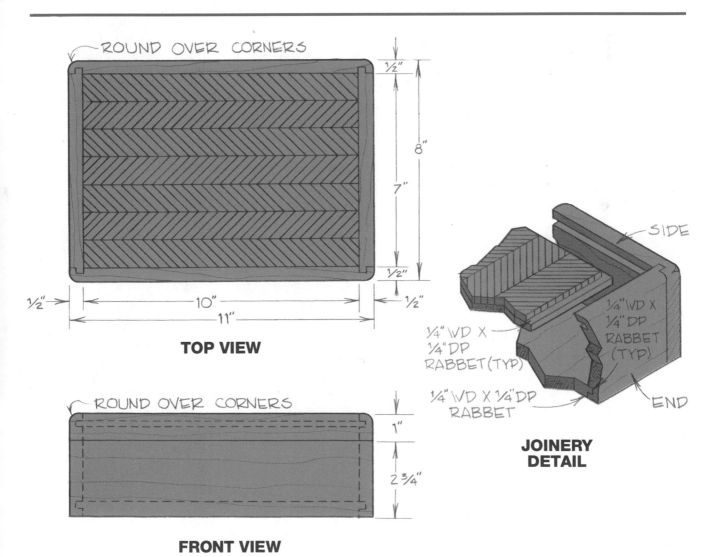

TOP VIEW

FRONT VIEW

JOINERY DETAIL

3 **Make the herringbone panel.** To make the herringbone panel, first cut the ³/₄″ plywood into ten 3″ x 10″ strips. Inspect the strips for voids. If a strip has a large void, discard that strip and make a new one. When you have ten void-free strips, glue them face to face. Let the glue dry for at least 24 hours. (See Figure 1.)

When the glue dries, sand one of the surfaces that shows the plies until it is clean and flush. Measure the distance between the inside faces of the sides on the test-assembled box. Draw a 1″-wide rectangle, *precisely* as long as the distance between the sides, at a 45° diagonal across the plies. Cut out this rectangle on a table saw, using a miter gauge and a miter gauge extension. (See Figure 2.) Test the fit of the rectangle between the sides — there should be no slop.

Slice this strip into smaller strips, each ¼″ thick. The plies should show on the *faces* of each strip, and they should run diagonally through the faces. (See Figure 3.) Flop half of the ¼″-thick strips so the plies are slanted in the opposite direction from the others. Position the strips edge to edge, so the slant alternates and the plies make a zigzag or herringbone pattern. Line up the strips so the veneer layers all meet. (See Figure 4.)

Carefully mark the strips so you can put them back together in the same order.

1/To make the herringbone stock, first glue up several strips of plywood, face to face. These strips must be relatively free of voids and other defects.

2/Cut a rectangular strip from the laminated plywood at a 45° diagonal. Attach an extension to the face of the miter gauge to hold the stock as you feed it into the saw blade. **Saw guard removed for clarity.**

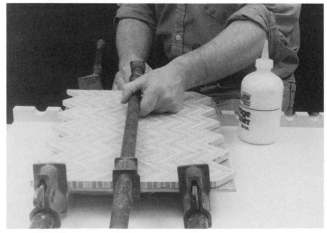

3/Slice the diagonal strip into ¼″-thick strips. The plies must show on the **face** of each strip. **Saw guard removed for clarity.**

4/Position the strips edge to edge so the plies form a zigzag pattern. The plywood veneer layers should match up.

4 **Assemble the box.** One by one, lay the herringbone strips in place on the top backing, making sure they fit the frame formed by the other parts. The fit should be fairly tight, both side to side and front to back. If it's too tight, you may have to sand a little stock from the edges of the strips. If it's too loose, you may have to cut a little stock from the ends of the sides, bringing the front and back closer together.

When you're satisfied that all the parts fit properly, disassemble them. Finish sand the front, back, sides, and bottom. Reassemble the parts with glue, wiping away any excess glue with a wet rag.

When the glue dries, sand the joints clean and flush. Also sand the herringbone strips flush with both each other and the top edges of the front, back, and sides.

5 **Round the corners of the box.** Using a hand-held router and a ³/₈″ quarter-round bit, round over the top edges of the front, back, and sides.

Also, round over the corners where the front and back join the sides. Sand the rounded corners to remove any mill marks.

6 **Make the lid.** Rip the lid from the box on a table saw, cutting the front and back first, then the sides. When you cut the last side, put several wedges in the kerfs to hold them open. Clamp the parts together to pinch the wedges in place. (See Figure 5.) If you don't use these wedges, the kerfs will close as you make the final cut, the saw will bind, and the mating edges of the lid and box will be uneven.

Mortise the adjoining edges of the back for hinges, then install the hinges with screws. If you wish to install a lid support, secure this to the inside surface of one side.

5/When ripping the lid from the assembled box, use wedges to keep the kerfs from closing as you make the final cut. Hold the wedges in place by pinching them in the kerf with clamps.

7 **Finish the box.** Remove the hinges and lid support. Do any necessary touch-up sanding on the wooden surfaces, then apply a finish. Coat the parts evenly, both inside and out. When the finish dries, rub it out. Apply a coat of wax and buff it. Finally, replace the hinges and the support.

Band-Sawed Boxes

There are many, many ways to make a box, but one of the most intriguing is to use a band saw — *exclusively.* By making carefully planned cuts in the proper order, you can saw the parts of a box from a solid block of wood. When you've finished cutting, you can reassemble these pieces so the completed box displays the same grain pattern and general shape as the original block. Using the band saw in this man-

ner, it's possible to make boxes from small logs, burls, glued-up scraps, and other interesting pieces of wood; these boxes will still look just as interesting, if not more so.

Shown are two styles of boxes you can make with a band saw. One has a single drawer, the other a locking lid. One was made from scraps of contrasting woods, glued up to make a solid block of many colors. The other was made from a burl.

They look very different from one another, and require a different series of band saw cuts. However, the end results are

similar in one respect: Both boxes preserve the general appearance of the block of wood from which they were cut.

Materials List

DIMENSIONS ARE NOT CRITICAL

PARTS

Box with Drawer

A. Box
B. Box sides (2)
C. Drawer front
D. Drawer bottom
E. Drawer sides/back

Box with Locking Lid

A. Box
B. Bottom
C. Lock
D. Lid

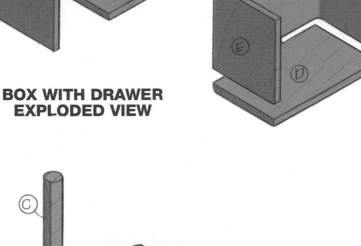

**BOX WITH DRAWER
EXPLODED VIEW**

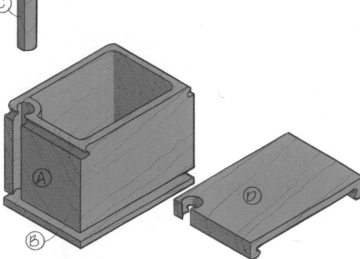

**BOX WITH LOCKING LID
EXPLODED VIEW**

Note: You can make either of these boxes almost any size you wish, depending on the size of the blocks you make them from. Furthermore, although you may follow the general contours of the cuts shown here, these will change from block to block. You'll have to change them to accommodate not only the size of the block, but also the shape, the grain pattern, and other distinctive features. The contours may also change with the kind and size of blade you use. For these reasons, we have included no dimensions in the Materials List or with the drawings. The list of parts and the patterns are meant to illustrate a technique only. Use your imagination to adapt this technique to wood blocks you wish to transform into boxes.

Making a Box with a Drawer

1 *Prepare the stock.* You can make a band-sawed box from *any* kind or species of wood you want, as long as it's dry. If you intend to make this box from laminated wood, glue stock together and let it dry for at least 24 hours. Sand or plane one flat surface on the wood block — that will become the bottom of the completed box. The other surfaces may be curved, flat, rough, smooth, or in between, depending on your preferences.

2 *Cut the drawer pull.* The drawer will need a pull so you can open it easily. You have several options for making this pull:

- You can choose a block of wood with a natural protrusion that will form a pull.
- You can attach a metal or wooden pull to the drawer front after making the box.
- You can cut or drill finger holes in the drawer front to serve as a pull.
- You can cut a pull into the front of the block with the band saw.

If you decide on the last option, you must make the pull now. This requires a sequence of eight cuts. First, mark where you want to cut the pull on the front of the block. Also, decide how far the pull will protrude from the front of the completed drawer. Attach a stop to the band saw table just *behind* the blade. This stop will halt the cuts so the finished pull protrudes the desired distance from the drawer front.

With the block resting on its bottom, make two cuts in the front, one on either side of the area that will become the pull. (See Figure 1.) Rest the block on its side, and make two more cuts. (See Figure 2.)

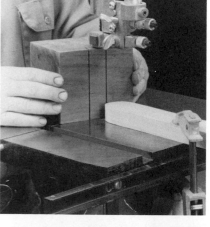

1/To make a drawer pull, first attach a stop to the worktable to halt the cuts at the proper depth. With the block resting on its bottom, make two cuts on either side of the area where you want to form the pull.

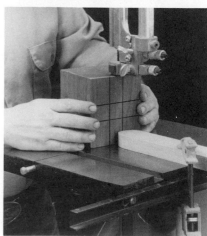

2/Turn the block on its side, and make two more cuts on either side of the pull area. The four cuts should form a grid, and they should all be exactly the same depth.

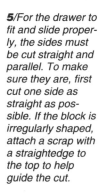

TRY THIS! If you make these first four cuts at a slight angle to the front of the block, so each cut runs in toward the center, the resulting pull will be slightly undercut. This will make it easier to grasp.

Remove the stop from the band saw table. With the block still resting on its side, cut in from the top and the bottom to remove the waste above and below the pull. (See Figure 3.) Turn the block back on its bottom and cut away the waste on either side of the pull. (See Figure 4.)

If you wish, carve the pull with a bench knife or shape it with a file, rounding or softening the corners.

3/Remove the stop from the worktable. With the block on its side, cut away the waste from above and below the pull.

4/Set the block on its bottom and cut away the waste on either side of the pull.

3 **Cut the sides of the box.** Slice off the sides of the block. These cuts must be perfectly straight and parallel to each other. If they're wavy, or if they draw closer at the front of the block, the drawer won't slide properly. If they draw closer at the back of the block, the drawer will fit sloppily when you pull it out. To be sure these cuts are parallel, attach a fence to the band saw after making the first side. Turn the block around so the surface you just cut rests against the fence. Then cut the second side, using the fence to guide the block. (See Figures 5 and 6.)

Note: The "case" — sides, top, bottom, and back of the box — should be no more than ¼" to ⅜" thick, if you can cut them this slender. This may not be possible, however, on a curved or irregularly shaped block. Make them as thin as the shape will allow.

5/For the drawer to fit and slide properly, the sides must be cut straight and parallel. To make sure they are, first cut one side as straight as possible. If the block is irregularly shaped, attach a scrap with a straightedge to the top to help guide the cut.

6/Attach a fence to the band saw table, turn the block around, and use the fence to guide the block as you cut the second side.

4 **Cut the drawer block.** Turn the block on one side to cut the drawer block. Like the sides, the top and bottom of the drawer must be straight and parallel. Adjust the position of the fence on the band saw, rest the bottom of the block against it, and cut the top of the drawer block. Carefully back the blade out of the cut, reposition the fence, and cut the bottom. (See Figure 7.) Remove the fence and cut the back of the drawer block freehand. (See Figure 8.)

7/To make sure the bottom and top of the drawer are straight and parallel, use the fence to guide the block as you make the cuts.

8/Remove the fence and cut the back of the drawer block freehand.

5 **Cut the drawer front.** Slice the drawer front from the drawer block. (See Figure 9.) You may freehand this cut; it's not particularly important that it be straight. However, you can use the fence to guide the cut, if you wish.

Note: The drawer front, sides, back, and bottom should be fairly thin — 1/8" to 1/4" thick.

9/Slice the drawer front (with the drawer pull, if you made one) from the drawer block.

6 **Cut the drawer bottom.** Cut the drawer bottom from the drawer block. (See Figure 10.) Once again, you can either cut this freehand or use a fence to guide the block.

10/Cut the drawer bottom from the drawer block.

7 Cut the drawer sides and back.
Finally, cut the drawer sides and back. (See Figure 11.) You can cut them using the same technique you used to make the box top, bottom, and back, if you wish — use the fence to guide the cuts for the two sides, then cut the back freehand. Or you can make all the cuts freehand; it's not critical that these cuts be straight or parallel.

11/Last, cut the drawer sides and back. Discard the waste.

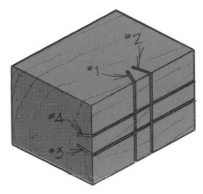

CUTS 1, 2, 3, AND 4 (STEP 2)

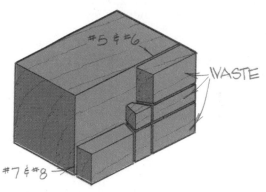

CUTS 5, 6, 7, AND 8 (STEP 2)

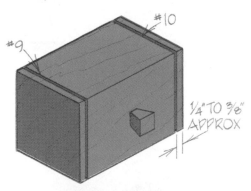

CUTS 9 AND 10 (STEP 3)

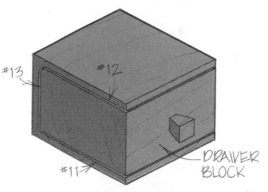

CUTS 11, 12, AND 13 (STEP 4)

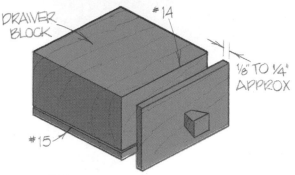

CUTS 14 AND 15 (STEPS 5 AND 6)

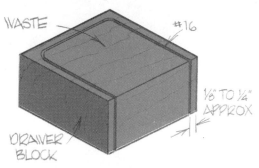

CUT 16 (STEP 7)

8 Assemble the box. *Lightly* sand all the cut surfaces. Remove as many of the saw marks as you can without taking away too much stock, or the drawer will fit sloppily. Too much sanding may also cause the drawer parts to fit poorly.

Glue the bottom of the drawer to the drawer sides and back, then glue the drawer front to the drawer assembly. Also, glue the box sides to the box top, bottom, and back. Wipe away any excess glue with a wet rag. When the glue dries, sand the joints clean and flush.

9 Finish the box and drawer. Insert the drawer in the box, then sand or file the front edges of the box flush with the drawer front. Finish sand the outside of the box, the drawer front, and the drawer pull. Remove the drawer and slightly round any hard edges or corners on the drawer front or inside the box opening. This will soften the appearance of the completed box.

Apply a *penetrating* finish, such as tung oil or Danish oil, to all wooden surfaces, inside and out, both box and drawer. Don't use a finish that builds up on the surface of the wood, like shellac or varnish — these may cause the drawer to stick. When the finish dries, secure a piece of felt in the bottom of the drawer with contact cement, if you wish. Then wax and buff the outside of the box and drawer.

Making a Box with a Locking Lid

1 Prepare the stock. Prepare the wood block in exactly the same way you did for the box with a drawer. If you intend to make this project from laminated wood, glue up the stock and let it dry thoroughly.

Sand or plane one flat surface on the wood block that will become the bottom of the completed box. The other surfaces may be flat, curved, or irregularly shaped — it makes no difference.

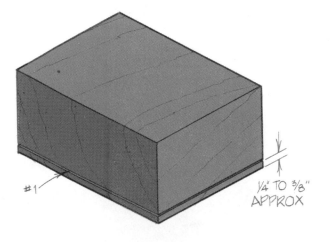

CUT 1
(STEP 2)

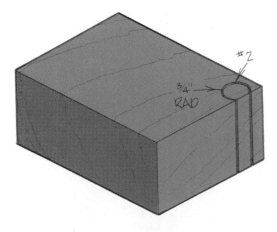

CUT 2
(STEP 3)

2 Cut the bottom of the box. Slice off the bottom of the block. The bottom should be about ¼"–⅜" thick. (See Figure 12.) You can freehand this cut, or use a fence to guide the block — it makes no difference.

12/The first step in making a box with a locking lid is to slice the bottom from the block. Cut the bottom ¼" – ⅜" thick.

3 Cut the lock. Cut the lock from the block freehand. (See Figure 13.) As shown, this lock is positioned on one end of the completed box, near a corner. However, you can put it anywhere you want along a side or an end. Also, the lock shown is round, but you can make it almost any shape. The only requirements are that it must nest securely in the cavity you cut it from, and that you *not* be able to remove it horizontally. It should be formed so you *have* to remove it vertically, from the top of the assembled box.

Note: You'll have to turn some tight corners when you cut the lock and the lid. Use a small band-saw blade — either ⅛" or 1/16" wide.

13/Cut the lock from a side or an end of the block. Use a small blade — either ⅛" or 1/16" wide — so you can make the lock as small and as unobtrusive as possible.

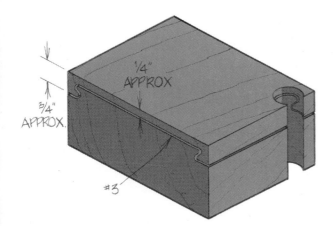

CUT 3
(STEP 4)

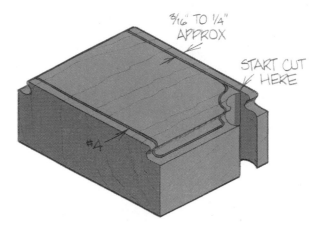

CUT 4
(STEP 5)

4 Cut the lid.

Cut the lid from the block free-hand. (See Figure 14.) Like the lock, this part can be cut to any shape, as long as it nests in or hooks on the assembled box. You shouldn't be able to lift the lid off vertically; you should have to slide it horizontally to remove it from the box.

14/Cut the lid from the block using a small, narrow blade as you did to make the lock. Like the lock, the lid must nest in or hook on the box.

5 Cut the sides and ends.

Lay out the inside shape of the box. The sides and ends should be slightly thinner than the bottom — 3/16"–1/4" thick. To remove the waste, start the cut inside the lock cavity. (See Figure 15.) Cut through to the layout line, then saw all around the inside of the block. (See Figure 16.)

TRY THIS!   Don't discard the waste! It may be large enough to make another, smaller box. In fact, if you start with a large enough block, you can make a set of nesting boxes.

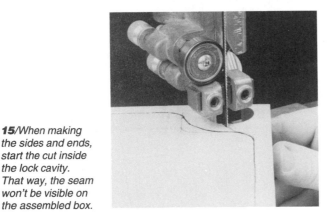

15/When making the sides and ends, start the cut inside the lock cavity. That way, the seam won't be visible on the assembled box.

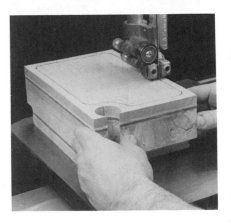

16/Cut through to the layout line, then continue the cut around the inside perimeter of the block.

6 Assemble the box.

Lightly sand all the cut surfaces. Remove as many of the saw marks as you can without taking off too much stock. If you sand too much, the lock and the lid will fit sloppily.

Glue the kerf in the box sides (the one you cut inside the lock cavity) to close it. When the glue dries, glue the bottom of the box to the box sides. Let this glue joint dry, then sand the joints clean and flush.

7 Finish the box, lid, and lock.

Slide the lid onto the box and insert the lock into its cavity. Sand or file all the outside surfaces flush. Finish sand the outside of the box, lid, and lock. Remove the lid and lock, then slightly round any hard edges or corners.

Apply a *penetrating* finish, such as tung oil or Danish oil, to all surfaces, inside and out. As before, don't use a finish that builds up on the surface of the wood. When the finish dries, reassemble the box, lid, and lock. Wax and buff the outside.

Corner Cupboard

Looking around for extra storage space? Look in the *corners* of your home. In many homes, the corners are vacant, waiting to be filled. The reason for this oversight is that most furniture is designed to stand in the center of a room or up against a wall. Corners are hard to use, and therefore often ignored.

A few types of storage furniture have been designed to make use of these vacant corners. One of the oldest and most popular is the corner cupboard — a large, triangular case with doors set at 45° to the walls. These pieces offer as much storage as conventional rectangular cupboards — sometimes more!

This contemporary country-style cupboard was designed and built by W. R. (Rick) Goehring, a professional cabinet-maker in Gambier, Ohio. Rick specializes in designing and building country-derived pieces such as this. He studies the country forms, particularly those of the Shakers, Moravians, Amish, and similar groups, then builds his own interpretations. ●

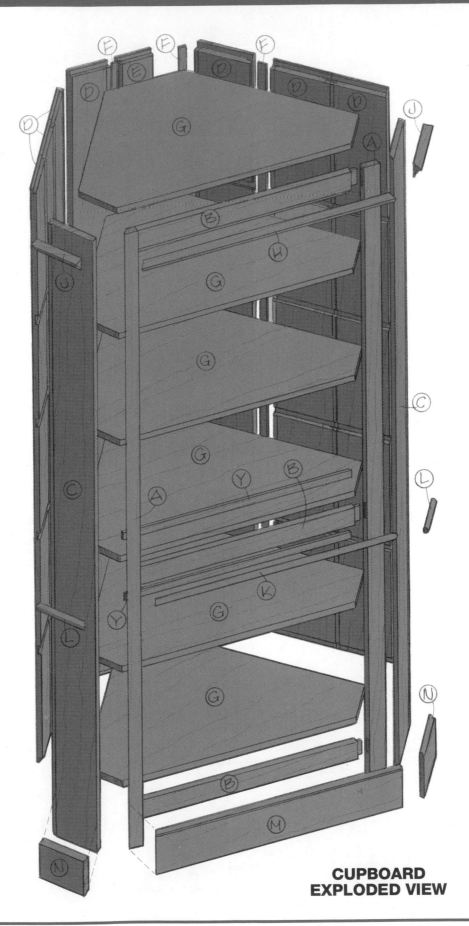

**CUPBOARD
EXPLODED VIEW**

Materials List

FINISHED DIMENSIONS

PARTS

A. Face frame stiles (2) — ³⁄₄″ x 2″ x 80″

B. Face frame rails (3) — ³⁄₄″ x 2¹⁄₄″ x 29⁷⁄₁₆″

C. Sides (2) — ³⁄₄″ x 6¹⁄₈″ x 80″

D. Wide backboards (7) — ³⁄₄″ x 6⁵⁄₈″ x 80″

E. Narrow backboard — ³⁄₄″ x 4¹³⁄₁₆″ x 80″

F. Splines (5) — ¹⁄₄″ x ³⁄₄″ x 80″

G. Shelves (6) — ³⁄₄″ x 17¹⁄₂″ x 39″

H. Front top molding — 1¹⁄₄″ x 1¹⁄₂″ x 32¹⁄₂″

J. Side top moldings (2) — 1¹⁄₄″ x 1¹⁄₂″ x 6⁵⁄₈″

K. Front middle molding — ³⁄₈″ x ³⁄₄″ x 31¹⁵⁄₁₆″

L. Side middle moldings (2) — ³⁄₈″ x ³⁄₄″ x 6³⁄₈″

M. Front bottom molding — ³⁄₄″ x 5″ x 32¹⁄₁₆″

N. Side bottom moldings (2) — ³⁄₄″ x 5″ x 6⁷⁄₁₆″

P. Outside top door stiles (2) — ³⁄₄″ x 2¹⁄₄″ x 41⁵⁄₈″

Q. Inside top door stiles (2) — ³⁄₄″ x 2¹⁄₂″ x 41⁵⁄₈″

R. Door rails (10) — ³⁄₄″ x 2¹⁄₄″ x 11⁵⁄₈″

S. Small top door panels (2) — ¹⁄₄″ x 9¹⁄₂″ x 10³⁄₁₆″

T. Large top door panels (2) — ¹⁄₄″ x 9¹⁄₂″ x 25⁹⁄₁₆″

U. Outside bottom door stiles (2) — ³⁄₄″ x 2¹⁄₄″ x 27⁷⁄₈″

V. Inside bottom door stiles (2) — ³⁄₄″ x 2¹⁄₂″ x 27⁷⁄₈″

W. Bottom door panels (2) — ¹⁄₄″ x 9¹⁄₂″ x 23¹³⁄₁₆″

X. Door pulls (4) — ³⁄₄″ dia. x 2³⁄₈″

Y. Door stops (3) — ³⁄₈″ x 1¹⁄₂″ x 31⁷⁄₈″

HARDWARE

1¹⁄₂″ x 2¹⁄₂″ Butt hinges and mounting screws (8)

Bullet catches (4)

#8 x 1¹⁄₄″ Flathead wood screws (60–72)

3d Finishing nails (12–18)

4d Finishing nails (¹⁄₄ lb.)

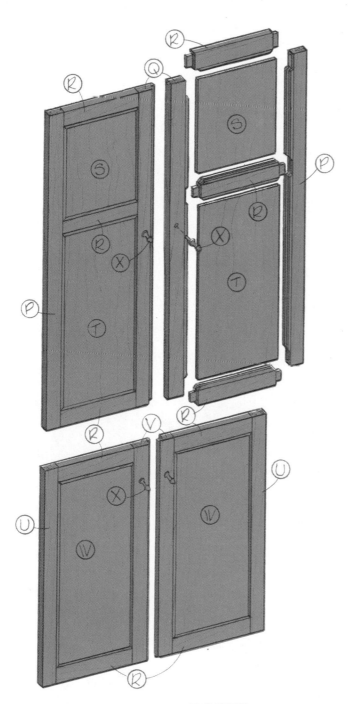

**DOORS
EXPLODED VIEW**

1

Select the stock and cut the parts to size. To make this project, you need approximately 95 board feet of 4/4 (four-quarters) stock and 3 board feet of 6/4 (six-quarters) stock. You can make this cupboard from almost any cabinet-grade wood, but country case pieces were traditionally made from walnut, cherry, or maple. The cupboard shown is made from cherry.

After selecting the stock, plane the 6/4 stock to 1¼″ thick. Resaw 5 board feet of the 4/4 stock in half and

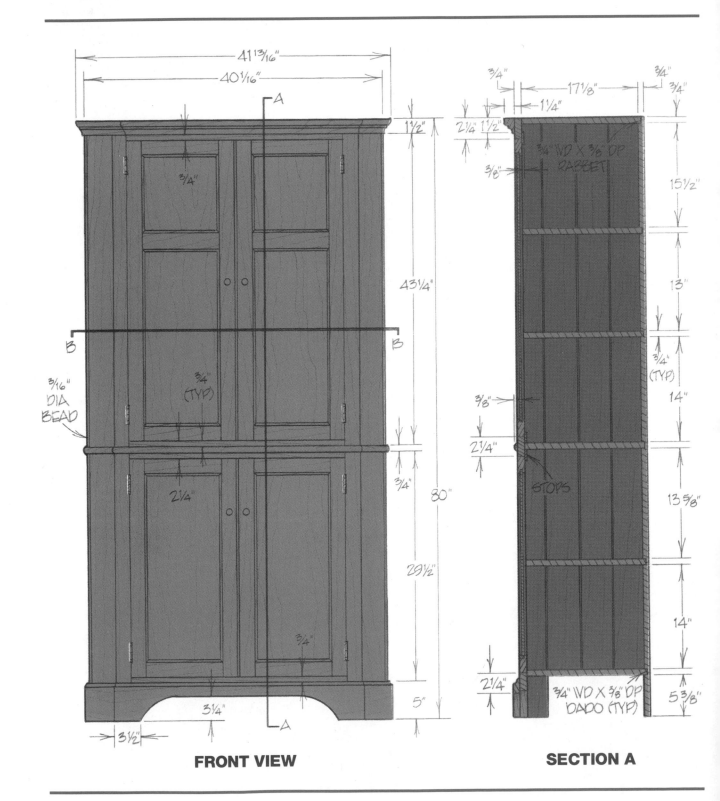

FRONT VIEW   **SECTION A**

plane it to ¼″ thick. Glue up the boards needed to make the wide door panels, but do *not* cut them to size yet. Plane the remaining 4/4 stock to ¾″, and glue up the stock needed to make the shelves. Cut the parts to the sizes shown in the Materials List *except* the mold-ings and door parts. (Wait until after you have assembled the case to cut these.) Bevel the adjoining edges of the backboards, sides, and face frame stiles at 22½°, as shown in *Section B*.

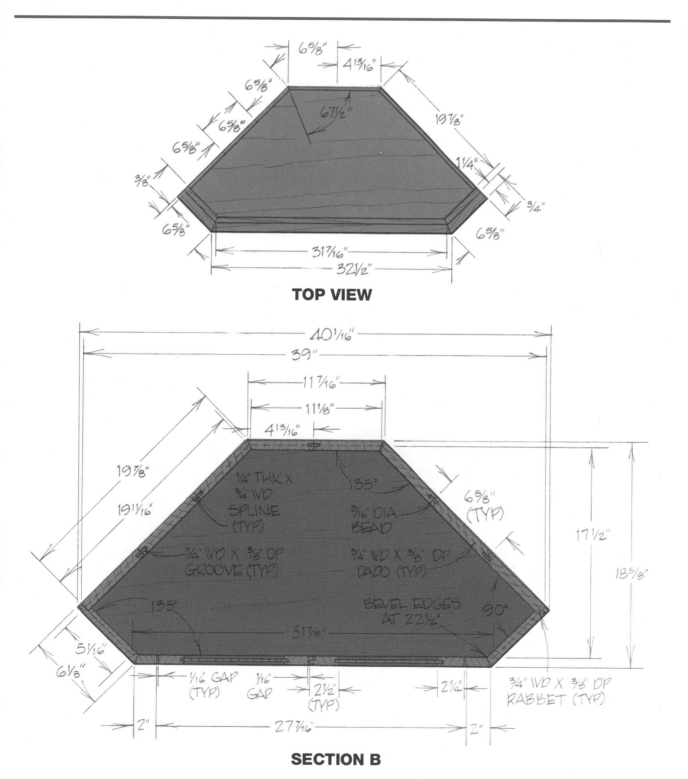

TOP VIEW

SECTION B

2 Cut the joinery in the sides and backboards.

The sides, backboards, and shelves are all joined with simple rabbets, dadoes, and grooves. Cut these joints with a dado cutter or table-mounted router:

- ³⁄₄″-wide, ³⁄₈″-deep rabbets in the back edges of the sides to hold the backboards, as shown in *Section B*
- ³⁄₄″-wide, ³⁄₈″-deep rabbets in the top ends of the sides and backboards to hold the top shelf, as shown in *Section A*
- ³⁄₄″-wide, ³⁄₈″-deep dadoes in the inside faces of the sides and backboards to hold the middle and bottom shelves
- ¹⁄₄″-wide, ³⁄₈″-deep grooves in the edges of the backboards to be splined

Note: When you cut the rabbets and dadoes that hold the shelves, make sure that these joints are positioned precisely the same from part to part. (See Figure 1.)

1/To make sure that the rabbets and dadoes in the sides and backboards are all cut precisely the same, *place the boards edge to edge on your workbench. Make sure the top and bottom ends are flush, then* *clamp the boards down. Cut the joints, routing across all the boards at once.*

3 Cut the mortises and tenons in the face frame members.

The face frame rails and stiles are joined with mortises and tenons. Cut the mortises first, then fit the tenons to them.

Lay out the mortises on the inside edges of the face frame stiles, as shown in the *Face Frame Layout*. Drill a 1³⁄₄″-long line of overlapping ¹⁄₄″-diameter holes to rough out each mortise, then clean up the sides and square the ends with a chisel. (See Figure 2.)

To make the matching tenons, cut a 1″-wide, ¹⁄₄″-deep rabbet in each end of each rail. These four rabbets will form a ¹⁄₄″-thick, 1³⁄₄″-wide, 1″-long tenon. (See Figure 3.) Make a tenon in a scrap first, and fit it to one of the mortises. If it's too loose, lower the cutter or the bit. If it's too tight, raise it.

2/When roughing out a mortise on a drill press, use a fence to guide the stock. This will keep the line of overlapping holes perfectly straight. Feed the bit slowly so it doesn't wander.

3/When cutting a tenon, score the shoulders on all four surfaces of the workpiece. Feed the wood slowly into the cutter or bit as you cut each surface. These two precautions will prevent the wood from chipping or tearing.

4 Cut the beads in the backboards and sides.

The adjoining edges of the backboards and the outside edges of the sides are cut with decorative beads, as shown in the *Backboard Joinery Detail* and *Section B*. Make these beads with a router, shaper, or molder. (See Figure 4.) You can also use a beading tool or "scratch stock" to make these beads. (See Figure 5.) These tools are available commercially, or you can make your own — refer to Making and Using a Scratch Stock, beginning on page 74.

4/If you use standard three-bead molding knives to cut a single bead, cover two of the beads with an auxiliary fence.

5/A beading tool or "scratch stock" looks like a spokeshave and works like a scraper. Draw the tool along the edge of the workpiece, pressing down gently. The blade will scrape the bead shape in the wood.

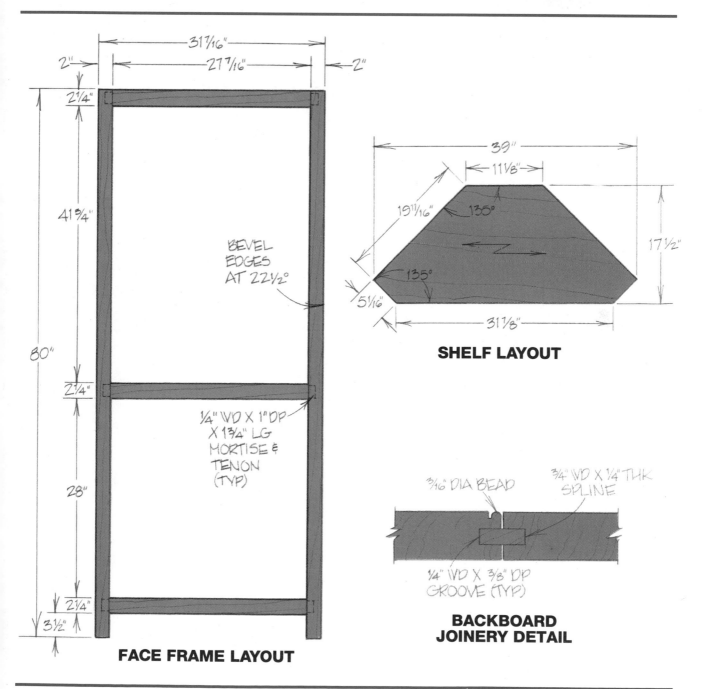

SHELF LAYOUT

BEVEL EDGES AT 22½°

¼" WD X 1" DP X 1¾" LG MORTISE & TENON (TYP)

3/16" DIA BEAD

¾" WD X ¼" THK SPLINE

¼" WD X ⅜" DP GROOVE (TYP)

BACKBOARD JOINERY DETAIL

FACE FRAME LAYOUT

5 Assemble the case.

Finish sand the shelves, backboards, sides, and face frame members — both the inside *and* outside surfaces. Glue the beveled edges of the face frame stiles to those of the sides, and the beveled edges of the side backboards to those of the rearmost backboards, making four separate assemblies. (See Figure 6.) When the glue dries, glue the backboards in the rabbeted edges of the sides.

With a helper, assemble the shelves and face frame rails to the other parts. Glue the tenons on the ends of the rails into the stile mortises. Slip splines between the backboards as you assemble them, and drive screws through the backboards and into the shelves. Countersink the heads of the screws.

Fasten the top shelf to the sides and backboards with 4d finishing nails, driving the nails down through the shelf and into the rabbeted ends of the other parts. Also fasten the face frame stiles and sides to the middle and bottom shelves with finishing nails. Position the nails in the middle of the case so they will later be covered by the middle moldings. Set the heads of the nails at the bottom of the case and cover them with putty. Sand all joints and surfaces clean and flush.

Note: Do *not* glue the shelves in the dadoes or rabbets. As these wide boards expand and contract, the

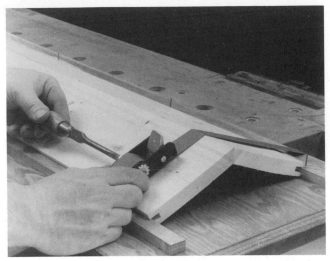

6/When gluing beveled parts edge to edge, make a simple clamping jig by nailing two long 1 x 1s to a wider board. This arrangement will keep the beveled parts at the proper angle to each other. Wrap band clamps or strips of old tire inner tubes around the jig and the parts while the glue dries.

screws and nails will flex slightly, but the case will remain square. If you glue these parts in place, the case may split or become distorted.

6 Make and install the moldings.

Cut the top and bottom molding stock to width, but not to length yet. Create the shapes in the moldings with a shaper or table-mounted router. Cut a $^3/_4$"-radius bead and a $1^1/_4$"-radius cove in the top molding parts, as shown in the *Top Molding Profile*. Cut an ogee in the top edge of the bottom molding, as shown in the *Bottom Molding Profile*.

To make the middle molding, round over an edge of a $^3/_4$"-thick board with a $^3/_8$" quarter-round bit or cutter. Then rip the rounded edge from the board, making a $^3/_8$"-thick half-round molding. (See Figure 7.)

Measure the outside of the assembled case. If the dimensions have changed from what is shown in the drawings, adjust the sizes of the moldings accordingly. Then cut the molding stock to length, mitering the adjoining ends at $22^1/_2$°.

Fasten the top and bottom moldings to the case with glue and screws, driving the screws from inside the case. Fasten the middle molding with 3d finishing nails. Set the heads of the nails, cover them with putty, and sand all surfaces clean and flush.

7/Rip the middle molding from a wide board **after** you cut the shape in the edge. Don't try to shape slender stock — it may splinter or break apart as you feed it into the cutter.

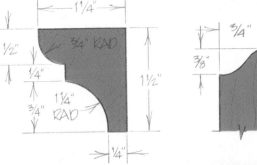

TOP MOLDING PROFILE

BOTTOM MOLDING PROFILE

7 Make the doors.

Make the doors. Measure the door openings in the assembled case. If the dimensions have changed from what is shown in the drawings, adjust the sizes of the door parts accordingly. (Note that when the doors are mounted in the case, there should be a $\frac{1}{16}''$ gap both between the doors and between each door and the face frame.) When you have refigured the dimensions, cut the parts to size.

As shown in the *Door Joinery Detail,* the door frames are assembled with $\frac{1}{4}''$-thick, $1\frac{3}{4}''$-wide, $1''$-long tenons and matching mortises. The panels float in $\frac{1}{4}''$-wide, $\frac{1}{4}''$-deep grooves, and the rails and stiles are decorated with $\frac{3}{16}''$ beads. Make the mortises, tenons, and grooves with a dado cutter or table-mounted router. Cut the beads with a molder, shaper, router, or scratch stock. (See Figures 8 through 13.)

Cut $\frac{1}{4}''$-wide, $\frac{3}{8}''$-deep rabbets in the *outside* edges of the *inside* door stiles, as shown in the *Door Overlap Detail.* Note that the rabbets must lap when the doors are closed. Make a bead in the outside surface of one stile and the inside surface of another, along the outside edges.

Finish sand the rails, stiles, and panels. Assemble the rails and stiles with glue, slipping the panels in place as you do. Do *not* glue the panels in the grooves; let them float. Make sure the door frames are square as you clamp the parts together. When the glue dries, sand the joints clean and flush.

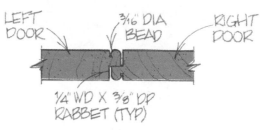

DOOR OVERLAP DETAIL

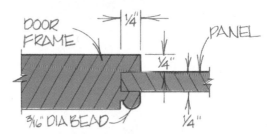

DOOR FRAME/PANEL JOINERY

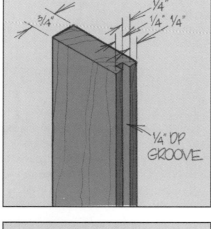

8/To make the door frames, first rout a $\frac{1}{4}''$-wide, $\frac{1}{4}''$-deep groove in all the **inside** edges of the rails and stiles.

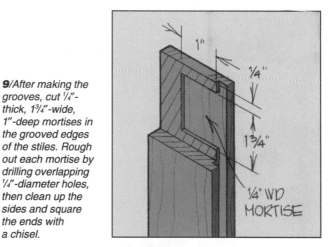

9/After making the grooves, cut $\frac{1}{4}''$-thick, $1\frac{3}{4}''$-wide, $1''$-deep mortises in the grooved edges of the stiles. Rough out each mortise by drilling overlapping $\frac{1}{4}''$-diameter holes, then clean up the sides and square the ends with a chisel.

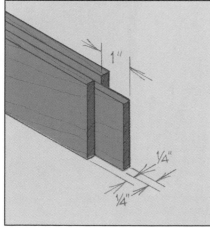

10/Cut $\frac{1}{4}''$-thick, $1''$-long tenons on the ends of the rails. These tenons should fit snugly (but not too tightly) in the mortises.

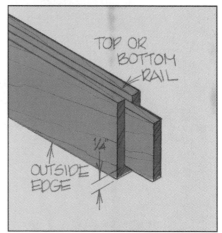

11/To fit the top and bottom tenons to the mortises, you must reduce their width by cutting a $\frac{1}{4}''$-deep notch or "haunch" in the outside edge of each tenon. The tenons on the middle rails of the top doors won't need to be notched — you have already reduced the width of these tenons when you cut the grooves.

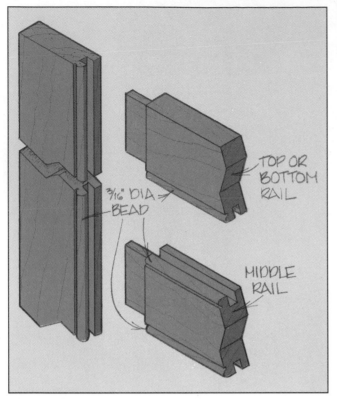

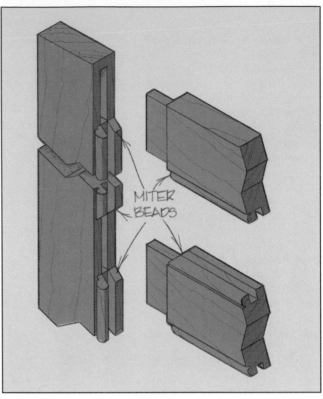

12/Cut decorative ³⁄₁₆" beads on the **outside** faces of the rails and stiles, along the **inside** edges.

13/Miter the sides of the grooves at 45°, where the rails join the stiles. When you assemble the parts of the doors, the beads should meet in a miter joint.

8 **Install the doors.** Measure the inside of the case, then cut the door stops to size, mitering the ends at 45°. Finish sand the stops and glue them to the inside of the face frame, as shown in *Section A*.

Mortise the doors and the face frame stiles for hinges. Attach the hinges to the doors with screws, then mount the doors on the cabinets. Install bullet catches in the top and bottom edges of the doors. (See Figure 14.)

Turn the door pulls on a lathe, as shown in the *Door Pull Layout*. Finish sand these pulls on the lathe. Drill ³⁄₈"-diameter holes through the door stiles to mount the pulls. Glue the pulls in the holes.

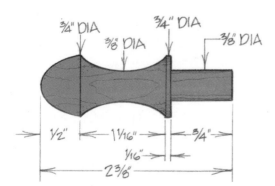

DOOR PULL LAYOUT

14/A bullet catch is a spring-loaded barrel with a ball at one end. To install a catch, drill a hole for the barrel in the edge of a door. Mortise the face frame for the plate. When the door is closed, the ball rests in the depression in this plate.

9

Finish the cupboard. Remove the doors from the cupboard and set the hardware aside. Do any necessary touch-up sanding to wooden surfaces, then apply a finish. Coat all surfaces evenly, both inside and out. This will help keep the case and the doors from warping or distorting. When the finish dries, rub it out. Apply a coat of wax and buff. Finally, replace the doors.

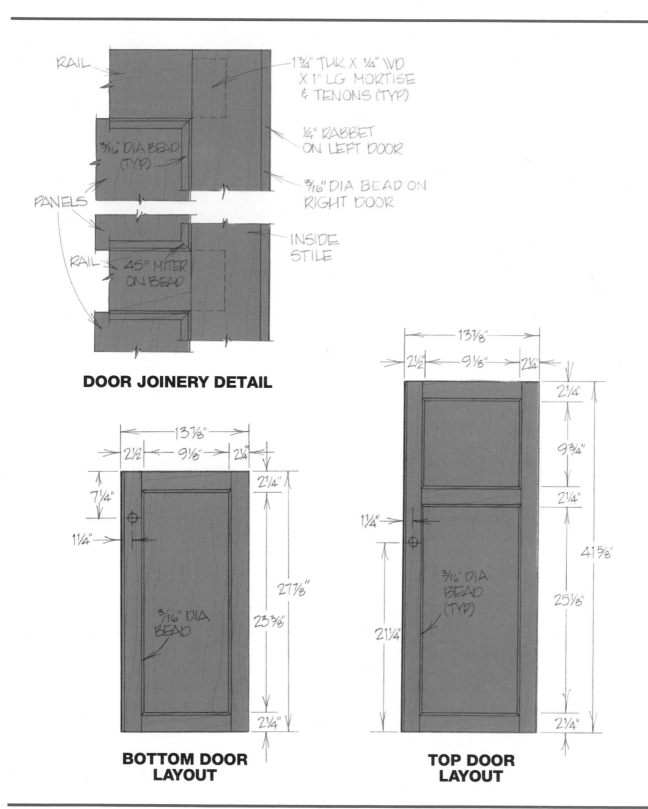

DOOR JOINERY DETAIL

BOTTOM DOOR LAYOUT

TOP DOOR LAYOUT

Credits

About the Author: Nick Engler is a contributing editor to *American Woodworker* magazine, and teaches wood craftsmanship and technology at the University of Cincinnati. He has written over 20 books on woodworking.

Contributing Craftsmen and Craftswomen:

Larry Callahan (Built-In Utility Cupboards, Pantry Wall)

Marian Curry (Wardrobe)

Nick Engler (Closet Organizer, Band-Sawed Boxes, Slide-Top Box, Wooden Briefcase, Photo Treasure Chest)

W. R. Goehring (Corner Cupboard)

David Hullinger (Quick Closet)

John Shoup (Herringbone Box)

David T. Smith (New England Mule Chest)

Note: Several of the projects in this book were built by woodworkers whose names have been erased by time. We regret that we cannot tell you who built them; we can only admire their craftsmanship. These include the Shaker Knife Box and Wooden Icebox.

The designs for the projects in this book (that are attributed to a designer or builder) are the copyrighted property of the craftsmen and craftswomen who made them. Readers are encouraged to reproduce these copyrighted projects for their personal use or for gifts. However, reproduction for sale or profit is forbidden by law.

Special Thanks To:
Chalmer and Delight Crowell
Gerlinde Lott
Don Sprowl
Wertz Hardware Store, West Milton, Ohio

WOODWORKING GLOSSARY

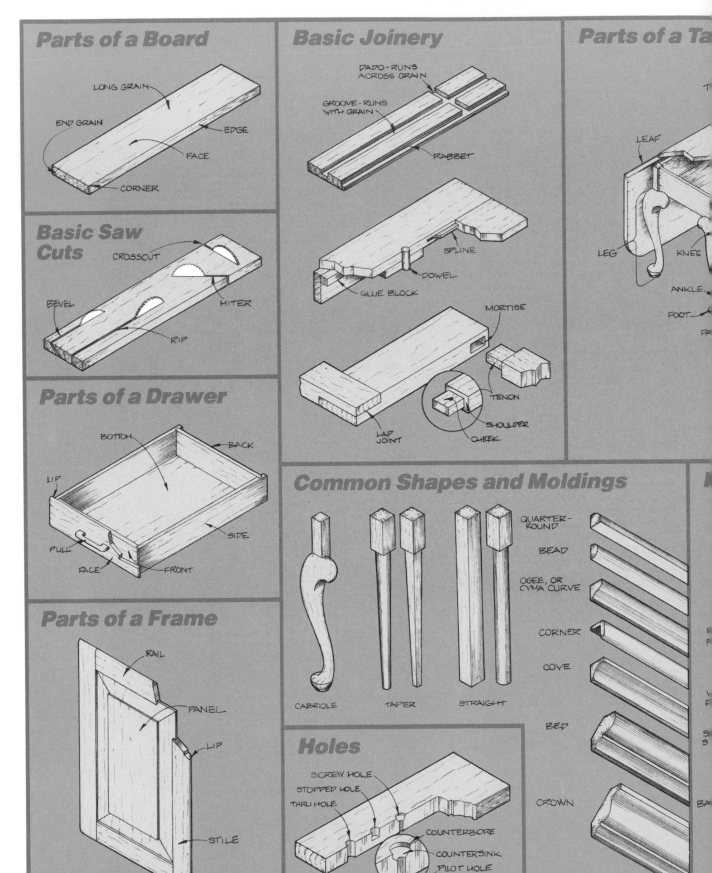

Parts of a Board

LONG GRAIN

END GRAIN

EDGE

FACE

CORNER

Basic Saw Cuts

CROSSCUT

BEVEL

MITER

RIP

Parts of a Drawer

BOTTOM

BACK

LIP

SIDE

PULL

FACE

FRONT

Parts of a Frame

RAIL

PANEL

LIP

STILE

Basic Joinery

DADO - RUNS ACROSS GRAIN

GROOVE - RUNS WITH GRAIN

RABBET

SPLINE

DOWEL

GLUE BLOCK

MORTISE

TENON

LAP JOINT

SHOULDER

CHEEK

Common Shapes and Moldings

QUARTER-ROUND

BEAD

OGEE, OR CYMA CURVE

CORNER

COVE

BED

CROWN

CABRIOLE

TAPER

STRAIGHT

Holes

SCREW HOLE

STOPPED HOLE

THRU HOLE

COUNTERBORE

COUNTERSINK

PILOT HOLE

Parts of a Ta

LEAF

LEG

KNEE

ANKLE

FOOT